Watchable Birds

of the

SOUTHWEST

Mary Taylor Gray

1995
Mountain Press Publishing Company
Missoula, Montana

Copyright © 1995
Mary Taylor Gray

Third Printing, February 1998

Front cover photograph (Gambel's quail)
copyright © 1995 Paul and Shirley Berquist

Front cover photograph (desert landscape)
copyright © 1995 Mary Taylor Gray

Back cover photograph (elf owl)
copyright © 1995 Paul A. Berquist

Each photograph copyright © 1995 by the photographer(s) listed in
the credit line: For a complete list of photo credits see page 180.

Excerpt on page 8 from *The Outermost House* by Henry Beston.
Copyright 1928, 1949 © 1956 by Henry Beston.
Copyright © 1977 by Elizabeth Beston.
Reprinted by permission of Henry Holt and Co., Inc.

Map page x copyright © by Sue Irwin/Eastside Desktop Publishing

Wetlands, Open Country, and High Country habitat icons
copyright © 1995 by Ed Jenne

Library of Congress Cataloging-in-Publication Data

Gray, Mary Taylor, 1955-
    Watchable birds of the Southwest / Mary Taylor Gray.
        p. cm.
    Includes bibliographical references (p.   ) and index.
    ISBN 0-87842-322-2 (pbk. : alk. paper)
    1. Birds—Southwest, New. 2. Bird watching—Southwest, New.
I. Title.
    QL683.S75G73 1995
    589'.0723478—dc20   95-34354
                                                     CIP

Printed in Hong Kong by Mantec Production Company

Mountain Press Publishing Company
1301 S. Third West • P.O. Box 2399
Missoula, Montana 59806

*To my husband, Rick Young, for his support,
his editing skills, and most of all his help and patience
in pursuing birds through the canyons and deserts of
the Southwest . . . when he could have been hiking!*

Contents

Foreword vii

Acknowledgments ix

Introduction 1
    How to Use This Book 3
    How to Watch Birds 6
    Wildlife-Watching Ethics and Etiquette 7

Selected National Parks
    and Monuments in the Southwest 9

Watchable Birds of the Southwest Species List 10

Birds of Wetlands:
    Rivers, Lakes, Streams, and Marshes 13

Birds of Open Country:
    Deserts, Grasslands, and Shrublands 61

Birds of the High Country:
    Mountains, Mesas, and Canyons 137

Southwest Birding Hotspots 177

Suggested Reading 179

Index 181

About the Author 187

Foreword

The United States is fast becoming a nation of birders. Birding has grown into a major, economically important pastime, attracting people from all walks of life, all age groups, and all levels of dedication. Over 60 million people birdwatch, spending billions of dollars in pursuit of their passion. The task before all of us now is to ensure that the objects of our birdwatching wonder are here to stay.

These days our feathered friends are not doing as well as they should be. Songbird populations are declining in numbers, creating a "silent spring" in our forests. Shorebirds face threats from coastal oil spills and beachfront development. Our majestic raptors are finding their forested winter homes in the tropics rapidly disappearing.

The colorful and melodious songbirds we took for granted for so long are now at a critical crossroads, and we face it with them. Increasing residential and industrial development, fragmentation of our once extensive forests and grasslands, and deforestation of tropical rain forests threaten our graceful flyers. If the environment fails to provide for the birds, then what can we expect for our own survival? Fortunately, we can do something about the problems now, before it becomes too late.

Significant partnership efforts are under way to stem the decline of our songbirds, shorebirds, and other nongame birds. The national Partners in Flight Program involves a contingent of federal, state, and private entities committed to the long-term survival of our neotropical birds. Partners in Flight concentrates on conserving those vibrant songbirds that bring music to our forests and grasslands: wood warblers, tanagers, thrushes, thrashers, grosbeaks, buntings, and sparrows.

The Western Hemisphere Shorebird Reserve Network is another successful conservation program created to protect important migration and wintering habitats for shorebirds in North and South America. These and other conservation initiatives are acting now to preserve our natural heritage before the "miner's canary" takes its last breath.

One agency or individual cannot do it alone—to ensure success requires willingness by everyone to participate in conservation. These programs forge partnerships with anyone willing to preserve our natural world. The dedication and expertise of individuals working together can prevent our songbirds and other nongame birds from becoming more sad statistics on the endangered species list, symbols of our failure to respond to their needs.

I can think of no one wanting to hike through a silent forest, to walk a beach without the company of sandpipers dodging the waves, or to gaze at an autumn sky and not see kettles of migrating hawks. Without them, we lose a piece of ourselves. Without them, can we not be far from our own demise?

Watchable Birds of the Southwest invokes awareness in anyone interested in birds and the natural world. This book is simple joy—showing us some of the most entertaining and unique birds found in the great Southwest. Additionally, by instilling understanding and appreciation for our wonderful assortment of birdlife, this book can further form partnerships among ourselves to ensure that our natural heritage stays with us and with future generations.

This book is for those of us enchanted with watching wildlife and who believe such pleasures in life are worth keeping.

JIM CLARK
CHIEF, BRANCH OF WILDLIFE TRAINING
NATIONAL EDUCATION AND TRAINING CENTER
U.S. FISH AND WILDLIFE SERVICE

Acknowledgments

Many thanks to the following photographers who donated their fine work to make this book "fly": Bryan Pridgeon, Steve Renzi, Terry Wygant, Chris Geanious, and especially Jim Clark for all his help and support, and for beautifully expressing the challenges facing birds—and all of us.

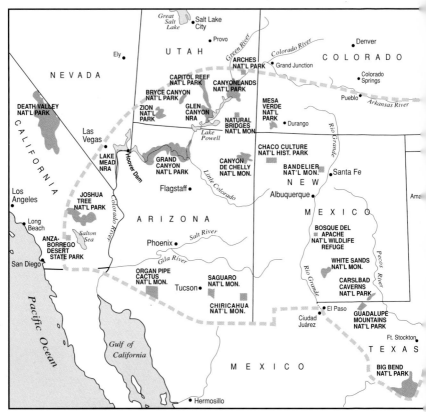

The Southwest. The dashed line surrounds the area covered in this book.

Introduction

To the casual observer, the deserts, canyons, and shrublands of the arid Southwest seem like wastelands devoid of life. How, after all, could anything live out there? Yet what seem like barren landscapes actually abound with a variety of birds, many specially adapted to life in the Southwest.

The Southwest is compelling country, with plunging cliffs and carved-rock canyons; wetlands and stream corridors, which are a delightful surprise; and deserts, bizarre lunar landscapes dotted with strangely shaped plants, all seemingly armed with spines. Before long, almost everyone, both visitor and resident, becomes intrigued with this land and its wildlife, particularly the birds. Have you been entertained by a pair of ravens swirling and diving above a steep canyon? Amused by a roadrunner perched atop your feeder? Perhaps a covey of Gambel's quail mills around your yard. Or maybe you've been enthralled by the wondrous flight of snow geese or the dance of sandhill cranes. If so, this book is for you.

Snow geese. –JIM CLARK

Watchable Birds of the Southwest, like its predecessor *Watchable Birds of the Rocky Mountains*, is written for families, tourists, nature lovers, armchair naturalists, and anyone who enjoys birds and the outdoors. You'll discover fun and intriguing tidbits about the "private lives" of the birds that are so much a part of the southwestern landscape. *Watchable Birds* will help you understand behaviors you observe and even tell you what some of these birds mean to Native Americans of the region. You'll read about funky and fascinating birds like the common poorwill, which you're not likely to see, but hearing it is a delight of the desert night. You may find you use *Watchable Birds* as a companion to a field guide, or you may just enjoy reading it even if you don't actually see a particular bird.

For some it may be a first step toward an interest in birdwatching, for others merely a source for basic information and interesting facts on birds of the region.

This isn't a field guide describing every possible species found in the Southwest, or even every *common* species. A comprehensive field guide can be overwhelming, causing the eyes of all but the confirmed

The saguaro cactus is the dominant tree in the Lower Sonoran Desert.
–MARY TAYLOR GRAY

birdwatcher to glaze over. Rather, this is a guide to those birds of the Southwest region that are particularly fun to watch because they're big, brightly colored, have interesting behaviors, or in some way particularly represent the Southwest. In other words, they're "watchable."

How to Use This Book

Birds are adapted to live in particular *habitats* that provide them with the food, shelter, water, and living space they need for their particular lifestyle. A duck obviously needs different things than a roadrunner or an eagle. Most people are not versed in the taxonomic groupings of species, but they can recognize the surrounding landscape, or habitat. Readers need only note which habitat they are in, then look within that section of the book for the bird they wish to read about. For simplicity's sake, the book "assigns" each species to the habitat it most typically inhabits. But birds are highly mobile; many don't frequent these habitats exclusively, so don't be surprised to see some of these birds showing up in other places.

For ease of use, the book groups the many habitats of the Southwest into three broad categories based on landscape features that are readily apparent.

Wetlands

Wetlands are home to species usually associated with water, be it lakes, ponds, marshes, rivers, or canyon streams.

Sandhill cranes at dusk, Bosque del Apache National Wildlife Refuge.
—MARY TAYLOR GRAY

3

You may think the Southwest is an arid land devoid of water, but major rivers such as the Colorado and Rio Grande flow through the region, fed by countless tributary streams that swell seasonally with mountain snowmelt and rain. The Sonoran Desert is in fact a fairly lush desert; visit it in spring and you'll marvel at the carpets of wildflowers and the fat stems of saguaro and other cacti, swollen with stored water. Many watered canyons support lush growths of sycamore and oak, or even harbor secret oases shaded by desert fan (or Washington) palms, the only palms native to the Southwest. Development, in the form of ranches, farms, housing subdivisions, resort communities, parks, and golf courses, also contributes a great deal of watered habitat for wildlife, often supporting species that previously would have had a hard time existing in the Southwest.

Open Country

This is a broad grouping, encompassing very diverse habitats—dry, low-elevation deserts dominated by cactus, agave, and yucca; shrublands where sagebrush, rabbitbrush, and other shrubs proliferate, as well as scattered small trees such as mesquite or paloverde; grasslands; and agricultural land including rangelands and old fields. Perhaps the easiest description is a land where you can see the horizon.

High Country

This area includes mountain forests, both coniferous and deciduous; stream-fed canyons; steep-walled, rocky canyons; and mesa tops.

Moving up from the desert through the mountains, you will notice the vegetation changing. Particular tree species dominate each of these "life zones." In a transition zone between desert and mountain lie the open woodlands of pinyon pine and juniper. These two small coniferous trees grow in close association with each other. This community, sometimes called the dwarf forest, is often referred to simply as "p-j."

Next is the pine-oak forest, where Gambel (or scrub) oak mingles with ponderosa pine. Higher up, Douglas fir and groves of quaking aspen are dominant. Finally, the highest zone before the treeless alpine tundra is the spruce-fir forest, with dense forests of Engelmann spruce and subalpine fir.

Red-tailed hawk atop
a saguaro cactus.
–MARY TAYLOR GRAY

Raven silhouettes. –CHRIS GEANIOUS

Wetlands scale: *hummingbird, sparrow, robin, crow, mallard duck, Canada goose, and eagle.*

Open Country and High Country scales: *hummingbird, sparrow, robin, crow, red-tailed hawk, Canada goose, and eagle.*

Anatomy of a Species Profile

Size: A graphic scale bears an arrow indicating the size of each species in relation to silhouettes of familiar birds. The birds on the scale are hummingbird, house sparrow, robin, crow, red-tailed hawk/mallard duck, Canada goose, eagle. These silhouettes are not drawn in accurate proportion to one another, but merely ranked in order from little to big. Remember that size can be difficult to judge because birds come in many shapes. Ducks, for example, have a horizontal posture whereas hawks sit upright. Herons look quite large, but most of their height is in the legs.

Name: Birds are listed by the American Ornithologists' Union (A.O.U.) accepted common name, followed by the two-part Latin name, shown in italics.

Family: This is the English family name as listed in *The Audubon Society Encyclopedia of North American Birds.*

A.K.A. (also known as): This lists other common names that may be more familiar to you.

Description: A brief description of the bird follows.

Natural History: This section offers information on the bird, its behavior, and how it lives its life. Here you'll find fun and interesting tidbits, the "I didn't know that" stuff.

Related species that you may also see in the Southwest are indicated in **bold**.

When and Where to See Them: This tells you what geographic area as well as in what habitat the bird is found at various times of year.

Eyecatchers: This section directs you to particular features or behaviors that will help you notice a species or distinguish it from other birds.

6

How to Watch Birds

Watching birds is lots more fun if you can identify them. A bird flits by, and you think you noticed enough detail to identify it, but upon checking a bird guide you find ten different birds that might fit. Training yourself to make a few mental notes when you glimpse a bird will help your identification.

Size. It's difficult to accurately judge the size of birds at any distance. Instead, judge size in relation to birds you know. Is it about the size of a sparrow? Is it bigger than a robin but smaller than a crow? To help you, this book indicates size in relation to familiar birds on a silhouette chart.

Shape. What is the general shape? Is the bird round and chunky like a sparrow or slender like a nuthatch? Make note of the shape of body parts—wings, tail, bill, legs. These will help you make some general associations. Owls have round heads; great blue herons have very long legs; ducks have "duck bills"; wrens have up-cocked tails. Characteristic traits also help differentiate between similar birds. Within the raptor family, for example, falcons have slender, tapering wings for fast pursuit in the air whereas hawks have wider wings for soaring.

Field Marks. Sometimes you have only a moment to glimpse a bird. Watch for noticeable features. Are there distinctive stripes, colors, or patterns on the bird? Is the breast spotted, are there stripes over the eyes, or white edges to the tail? Do patches under the wings or on the tail "flash" when the bird flies? You may notice a crest, but is it pointed like a cardinal or more sloping like a kingfisher?

Posture/Position. The perch or setting in which you see a bird gives clues to its lifestyle. Is it gripping the trunk of a tree, perched on a tree limb, hopping on the ground, or wading in the shallows? Also notice its posture. Is it sitting upright or holding its body parallel to the ground?

Voice. Bird song fills the natural world with life and joyful music. Becoming familiar with a bird's song is not only a pleasure but also a clue to who's in the neighborhood—even if you can't see them.

Habitat. Don't just note what a bird looks like. Realize where it lives to give you clues to its identity. Are you in a woodland or meadow or is the bird close to, or in, water?

Wildlife-watching Ethics and Etiquette

When watching birds remember that you are in essence entering the animals' "home" and should conduct yourself as a guest. Respect the animals and don't disturb them, their nests, or their habitat. Don't approach any closer than the birds feel comfortable. If they alter their behavior, stop feeding, or otherwise seem agitated, back off. Obviously if a bird flushes or flies off, you won't get a very good look anyway.

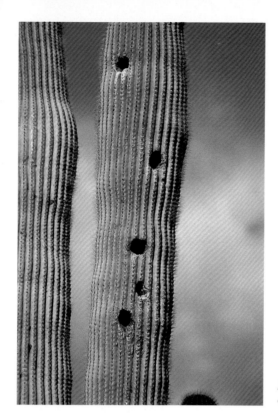

Nest holes in a saguaro cactus. –MARY TAYLOR GRAY

Never chase, feed, handle, or disturb animals. When you go out birdwatching, leave your pets at home.

We've all seen close-up photos of hawks or eagles with the bird puffed up in a threatening posture, its beak open in a threat gesture. That photographer approached too closely and threatened the bird. Intrusion into a bird's living space can expose it to predation, keep it from feeding or other essential activities, or cause it to leave or abandon its nest, exposing eggs or chicks to predation or the elements. No photo or viewing opportunity is worth harassing or stressing wildlife. In appreciating and watching birds and other wildlife, we have a responsibility to protect and preserve the animals that share our world.

> *We need another and a wiser and perhaps a more mystical concept of animals. . . . In a world older and more complete than ours they move finished and complete, gifted with extensions of the senses we have lost or never attained, living by voices we shall never hear. They are not brethren, they are not underlings; they are other nations, caught with ourselves in the net of life and time, fellow prisoners of the splendour and travail of the earth.*
>
> —*The Outermost House*, Henry Beston

Selected National Parks and Monuments in the Southwest

Arizona
Canyon de Chelly National Monument
Chiricahua National Monument
Grand Canyon National Park
Organ Pipe Cactus National Monument
Saguaro National Monument

California
Joshua Tree National Park

Colorado
Mesa Verde National Park

Nevada
Lake Mead National Recreation Area

New Mexico
Bandelier National Monument
Carlsbad Caverns National Park
Chaco Culture National Historic Park
White Sands National Monument

Texas
Big Bend National Park
Guadalupe Mountains National Park

Utah
Arches National Park
Bryce Canyon National Park
Canyonlands National Park
Capitol Reef National Park
Glen Canyon National
     Recreation Area (Lake Powell)
Natural Bridges National Monument
Zion National Park

Watchable Birds of the Southwest
Species List (68 species total)

Wetlands

Pied-billed grebe
Great blue heron
Snowy egret
Green heron
Snow goose
Canada goose
Green-winged teal
Mallard
Northern pintail
Cinnamon teal
Bald eagle
Northern harrier
Common moorhen
Sandhill crane
Killdeer
Belted kingfisher
Black phoebe
Vermilion flycatcher
Red-winged blackbird
Summer tanager

Open Country

Turkey vulture
Red-tailed hawk
American kestrel
Scaled quail
Gambel's quail
Inca dove
Mourning dove
Greater roadrunner
Great horned owl
Elf owl
Burrowing owl
Lesser nighthawk
Common poorwill
Black-chinned
　hummingbird
Costa's hummingbird
Gila woodpecker
Western kingbird
Horned lark
Cactus wren
Northern mockingbird
Curve-billed thrasher
Phainopepla
Loggerhead shrike
Northern cardinal
Pyrrhuloxia
Blue grosbeak
Black-throated sparrow
White-crowned sparrow
Western meadowlark
Great-tailed grackle
Hooded oriole
House finch

High Country

Golden eagle
Peregrine falcon
Wild turkey
White-throated swift
Acorn woodpecker
Cliff swallow
Steller's jay
Gray-breasted jay
Common raven
Bridled titmouse
White-breasted
　nuthatch
Canyon wren
Western bluebird
Yellow-rumped
　warbler
Painted redstart
Dark-eyed junco

—MARY TAYLOR GRAY

BIRDS OF WETLANDS

Rivers, Lakes, Streams, and Marshes

Pied-billed grebe
Great blue heron
Snowy egret
Green heron
Snow goose
Canada goose
Green-winged teal
Mallard
Northern pintail
Cinnamon teal
Bald eagle
Northern harrier
Common moorhen
Sandhill crane
Killdeer
Belted kingfisher
Black phoebe
Vermilion flycatcher
Red-winged blackbird
Summer tanager

Pied-billed Grebe

Podilymbus podiceps

A.K.A.: hell diver, water witch, dabchick

Family: Grebe

This grebe is a small, brown, tail-less water bird with a round head and chickenlike bill. During breeding season, the adults have a black ring around the bill and a black chin. In winter the neck is reddish.

Natural History: The charming little pied-billed grebe moves effortlessly around a pond like a round rubber ducky. Suddenly the grebe bobs underwater with barely a ripple. The watcher waits with anticipation for the bird to reemerge—will it surface here, or there? Then up pops the grebe with a bit of vegetation in its bill, only to duck underwater again a moment later. Frightened by an intruder, a grebe sinks slowly below the water's surface until only its head remains above water like a periscope. Like their larger, more elegant-looking cousins the **western grebes,** pied-billed grebes build floating nests that they anchor to pond vegetation. The chicks ride along on the backs of their parents when the adults head out to feed. When the parent dives, the young go along too, hanging on to the adult's feathers with their bills. This little grebe's diving behavior has earned it nicknames like hell diver and water witch.

The pied-billed is the most widespread of North American grebes. It is mainly a meat eater, consuming insects, snails, fish, tadpoles, and occasionally seeds and parts of water plants. Pied-billed grebes are usually solitary and breeding pairs are somewhat secretive.

When and Where to See Them: On lakes, ponds, and marshes with fairly heavy vegetation.

Eyecatchers

Watch for the grebe's charming fishing style as well as its small size and lack of tail. The grebe swims along peering left and right, then, looping its neck in a sudden dive, it disappears underwater, to pop up again unexpectedly.

14

The little pied-billed grebe, with its snub nose and bobbed tail, may suddenly disappear underwater, only to surface elsewhere.

Great Blue Heron

A.K.A.: blue crane

Ardea herodias

Family: Heron

Standing up to four feet tall, this gray-blue wading bird has a long neck, stilt legs, and spearlike bill. A plume of blue or black feathers trails from its head. Breeding adults have feathery plumes on the chest.

Natural History: The great blue heron is a familiar inhabitant of ponds and marshes, yet always a joy to watch. Poised motionless in the shallows, it seems to embody serenity and patience. Yet the heron is eyeballing creatures below the water's surface, be they fish, frog, or crayfish, with its telescopic vision. Suddenly the bird plucks a morsel from the water with its spearlike bill. If the meal is bulky enough, you may see its outline move slowly down the heron's skinny throat.

With their huge wing spans, deliberate movements, and reptilian design, great blue herons often seem like flying reptiles slowly circling a primordial swamp. Using their opposable toe, they may perch in the upper branches of trees, their large shapes looking oddly out of place.

This ability to roost in trees like songbirds allows great blues to build large stick nests high in cottonwoods and other trees along the water's edge. Circling in to land, they settle in the treetops in an awkward folding of long stick legs, large wings, and snakelike neck. Great blues nest in colonies, their many nests visible as messy clumps among the upper branches. Heronries are a riot of bird activity and noise—the rattle of wings, the rustle of feathers, the cackles of nestlings, and the croaking calls of the adults. Herons use the same nest sites year after year until the trees holding the nests die and become unstable, threatening entire nesting colonies. The occasional dry-land heron nest is an oddity.

When and Where to See Them: Year-round on marsh-lined lakes, ponds, streams, canals, and wetlands. Heronries require trees in protected sites over or near water to support the large nests.

Eyecatchers

A large gray-blue bird stands motionless in the shallows of a pond or slow-moving stream. In flight, notice the very large, slightly cupped and slowly flapping wings. Herons fly with their necks curved back in an S shape and their long legs held out behind.

16

Leg color helps distinguish the snowy egret (above) from the cattle egret (below). For the breeding season, the cattle egret develops orange plumage on its head and chest.

Green Heron
**A.K.A.: little green heron,
green-backed heron**

Butorides virescens
Family: Heron

This is a small, short-legged heron with coppery breast, green back, and white neck and throat. Like the black-crowned night-heron, the green heron has a short neck, which gives it a "no-neck" appearance.

Natural History: It may require extra attention to notice the motionless green heron poised at the water's edge. Because of its plumage color, the green heron blends into its surroundings even more than other herons. When hunting, green herons stalk slowly in the shallows or hang out waiting for prey to happen by, often perched on a low-hanging limb or on the shore. Sometimes they must get tired of waiting. Shuffling their feet in the mud, the herons send crayfish and other prospective dinner items scurrying from their hiding places in the sediment, to be nabbed by the heron's sharp bill. When excited, a green heron raises its crown feathers. In defending its home turf, the green heron opens its mouth to show the bright red lining.

Unlike many other herons, green herons are fairly solitary, often fishing alone. While great blues and black-crowned night-herons are known for their large, raucous colonies, green heron pairs usually nest in a tree away from others.

When and Where to See Them: In the shallows along ponds, lakes, and marshy areas from early spring through midautumn. They nest in trees near water.

Eyecatchers

You'll know this heron by its lovely green and copper color.

The green heron is shy, making it difficult to approach. –JIM CLARK

Snow Goose
A.K.A.: blue goose (dark phase)

Chen caerulescens
Family: Duck

This handsome goose is dazzling white, with black wingtips, pinkish legs and bill, and black "lipstick" on the bill edge. The dark-phase blue goose is dark gray with white head.

Natural History: To see the flight of the snow goose is to witness one of the premier sights of nature. Gathering in great flocks of thousands, the white, sleek-necked geese are a wonder. While the Canada goose's two-toned honk is a familiar call, the snow goose's voice is more a high-pitched, cacophonous honking as an entire flock sounds off together. Like Canada geese, snows feed on grass, aquatic plants, and cultivated grains left in fields after harvest.

Winter is the season for snow geese in the Southwest, and the Bosque del Apache National Wildlife Refuge near Socorro, New Mexico, is the best place to witness their incredible spectacle. As many as 100,000 snow geese winter in the area. At dawn the geese begin to stir, getting up in small groups to move from the safety of the water to surrounding grain fields to feed. Watching them from the edge of the ponds is a bit like sitting on the runway of a busy airport. Groups of geese fill the sky all around you, some taking off here, others landing over there. In late afternoon and evening, trailing lines of white geese mark the sky as the birds return. They settle on the refuge's ponds in great numbers, like white feathers shaken from a down pillow.

By late winter the snow geese begin the long migration north to their nesting grounds on the barren Arctic tundra.

When and Where to See Them: Bosque del Apache National Wildlife Refuge (south of Albuquerque, NM) from November through March (best time—December through February). Some birds may be seen in migration on ponds and open water.

Eyecatchers

Large flocks of snowy white geese with black wingtips, sounding a cacophony of high-pitched honking, can't be missed. Note how they fly in trailing lines or in U formation, not in a crisp V like Canada geese.

22

The "blue goose" (right) is a dark plumage phase of the snow goose. —BRYAN H. PRIDGEON
Snow goose showing the black "lipstick" on its bill. —BRYAN H. PRIDGEON

Bosque del Apache National Wildlife Refuge is an important wintering area for thousands of snow geese. —JIM CLARK

Canada Goose
A.K.A.: honker

Branta canadensis
Family: Duck

You can't mistake the Canada with its long black neck, black head with white chinstrap, large size, and wonderful honking call.

Natural History: Over most of North America, the haunting honk of "goose music" is the voice of autumn. Who isn't compelled to look skyward when trailing V's of Canada geese pass overhead, sounding their call? Unlike many members of the duck family, geese choose a mate for life, staying with each other year-round and caring solicitously for their babies. Canadas are early nesters; a late spring storm may find the female steadfastly incubating her eggs even as the snow falls on her back. Spring and early summer find the goose family swimming together on ponds and lakes, the long-necked parents sailing serenely, with a line of fluffy, yellow-and-black babies trailing behind.

Geese are great fun to watch. A foraging flock is watched over by sentinels. On water, the flock never seems to notice danger yet always glides effortlessly just out of harm's way. But on land, intruders approaching too close are met by an angry, hissing goose with lowered head and extended neck. To the human observer this seems to be the same display used during courtship. The male approaches his intended with neck extended and head lowered, except his intent is mating, not aggression, and in this display he entwines his neck with hers.

Mated pairs of geese form long-term bonds. Listen closely the next time a flock flies over. The two-toned *ho-onk* is given by each pair—one sounding first, its mate answering a note lower.

When and Where to See Them: On ponds and open water year-round through much of the Southwest, moving into more northern regions for summer nesting.

Eyecatchers

Listen for the resonant, two-toned honking of the Canadas.

Canada goose with a trailing parade of goslings brings delight to spring birdwatching. –JIM CLARK

Green-winged Teal

A.K.A.: common teal, greenwing, red-headed teal, mud teal

Anas crecca
Family: Duck

A small, gray-brown duck with a green patch on the wing, the male has a red head with an emerald green stripe. The female is a drab, speckled brown.

Natural History: Side by side on a pond or dabbling in the shallows, a pair of little green-winged teals moves about, bobbing like two dinghies. When swimming on the same pond with a mallard, the compact teal makes its cousin look like a great lumbering boat. But it's in the air that green-winged teals really strut their stuff. The airborne flock wheels and banks, swoops down to scope out a pond, then zips upward only to bank again, all flying together in tight formation.

Curiously, this fine flier and swimmer often covers a fair distance on land searching for food. Aquatic vegetation and invertebrates are the mainstay of dabbling ducks, but greenwings also eat waste grain in fields and move into meadows and woods for berries, nuts, and acorns.

Ducks always afford birdwatchers a treat in spring with their courtship antics. The male greenwing's distinctive courtship call—*KRICK-et*—gives this duck its Latin name. After mating, the male leaves the female to incubate the eggs and rear the young on her own. Greenwings are among the first migrants to return north in spring; in mild winters, many don't migrate, as long as they can find sufficient open water to feed and seek shelter from predators.

Greenwings are the smallest of North American ducks and one of the most common. Despite their size, green-winged teals are popular game birds. Accounts from the nineteenth century, before bag limits, report individual hunters shooting more than 70 a day.

When and Where to See Them: In winter through most of the Southwest on lakes, ponds, and waterways. They occasionally nest in northern New Mexico and along Arizona's Mogollon Rim.

Eyecatchers

The male's red head displays a handsome green stripe curving from the eye down along the head.

Male green-winged teal. –MARY TAYLOR GRAY

▲

Mallard
Anas platyrhynchos
A.K.A.: greenhead, curlytail
Family: Duck

A very familiar large gray duck, the male mallard has a shiny green head with a white neck ring. The female is a nondescript brown.

Natural History: Mention the word *duck* to anyone and the likely image is of the beautiful and familiar mallard. Found throughout the world's temperate regions, the mallard is the ancestor of all domestic ducks except the Muscovy. The iridescent, emerald head of the mallard drake is a familiar sight throughout the Southwest—on waterways, golf courses, ponds, or wherever there is shallow open water. In contrast to her showy mate, the female mallard is dressed in basic brown, difficult to distinguish from many other female ducks. As dabbling or puddle ducks, the mallards tip "bottoms-up" when feeding to reach plants and other detritus below the water's surface. This feeding strategy leaves a busy pond dotted with duck tails pointing toward the sky.

Mallard courtship is entertaining to watch. The drake shows himself off by raising his wingtips, tail, and head in a "head-up, tail-up" display. He also gives a "grunt-whistle": scooping up water, bowing his head to his breast, then whistling and spouting the water toward the object of his courtship. The female does an "inciting display" to provoke her suitor to attack other males, perhaps to judge their suitability as mates. She swims toward a group of males with neck outstretched and head just above the water or, when a strange male approaches, swims after her mate, quacking and flicking her head sideways. Females are also the ones doing the quacking, a loud *QUACK, Quack, quack, quack,* decreasing in pitch.

During the breeding season, the mated pair are monogamous, but the drake leaves the hen to single parenthood soon after she lays the eggs. Within 24 hours of hatching, the downy ducklings follow their mother to water, trailing her in and out of the reeds.

When and Where to See Them: Year-round on open water, puddles, streams, or wherever there's a bit of standing water.

Eyecatchers

The mallard drake has a gleaming, emerald head.

Male mallard. –JIM CLARK

The female mallard's drab plumage (center) contrasts sharply with the male's flashy plumage. –TERRY WYGANT

Northern Pintail

A.K.A.: sprig tail, pheasant duck, gray duck, picket-tail, sea wigeon

Anas acuta
Family: Duck

The male pintail is a handsome bronze-brown duck with a white stripe on the side of the head extending down the underside of the neck. The head is a solid brown and the body a mottled gray-brown. A few long, black feathers protrude from the tail. The female is a drab mottled brown and lacks the exaggerated tail.

Natural History: Pintails range throughout the Northern Hemisphere and are one of our most common North American ducks, second only to mallards. Their numbers are estimated in the millions. Whether you see a handful of pintails or a lake covered with a raft of them, watch them bob gracefully with their arrow tails held high.

The pintail pair "meets" and bonds during winter; the male then follows the female to her nesting ground. A fickle mate, he departs soon after the eggs are laid and seeks out other females for mating.

Pintail females often build their nests in exposed areas concealed by grass and stubble. If an intruder ventures too near her nest, she will feign injury to draw the trespasser away from her nest.

Pintails appear on field puddles and temporary bodies of water to forage, moving on when these dry up. They seem particularly sociable with mallards, and the two species occasionally interbreed.

Pintails feed in the mud of shallow ponds, tipping to gobble bits of plants and detritus. Ninety percent of their diet is plant material. Because of this feeding strategy, they often ingest great amounts of spent lead shot, built up over the years in pond sediment. Pintail and other waterfowl populations suffered heavily from lead shot poisoning. Since the late 1980s federal law has required the use of steel shot to protect waterfowl.

When and Where to See Them: On marshes and ponds, September through April in southern New Mexico, California, Texas, and most of Arizona; year-round through the rest of the Southwest.

Eyecatchers

Look for a long "pin tail"—pointed feathers angling up from the tail—and a white throat contrasting with brown plumage.

30

Male pintail.

Pintails take flight in an eruption of flapping, splashing, and honking.

Cinnamon Teal

A.K.A.: red teal, river teal

Anas cyanoptera

Family: Duck

The male is a small, beautiful duck with gleaming, cinnamon-red plumage. Like most ducks the female is a nondescript brown, almost indistinguishable from other teal species.

Natural History: A small dabbling duck, the cinnamon teal is more shy in its habits than its more common cousins, the blue-winged teal and mallard. While the mallard has adapted well to human neighbors, the cinnamon teal is less tolerant of human encroachment, and its populations have declined with development and the draining of wetlands.

Cinnamon teal aren't usually seen in large flocks, preferring instead to travel in pairs. Unlike some other ducks, the male cinnamon maintains its bond to the female while she is on the nest. They build their nests in grass-lined depressions in a marshy area or meadow near water. Cinnamon teal nests are sometimes parasitized by other duck species, like redheads, mallards, and ruddy ducks. These ducks lay their eggs in teal nests, leaving their young to be raised by the diminutive cinnamon teal female. Cinnamon teals are the only waterfowl to breed in both North and South America and are rare east of the Rocky Mountains.

Ducks were important birds to the Pueblo peoples, who saw them as travelers and searchers, wise in the ways of many worlds—on the earth, in the sky, and below the water. Ducks were thought to carry things back and forth from the north on their annual migrations. Spirits returning home, it was believed, took the form of ducks.

When and Where to See Them: In summer on marshes, ponds, and open water. Year-round in parts of southern California, southwestern Arizona, and southern New Mexico.

Eyecatchers

In the sun the male cinnamon teal glows like burnished copper.

32

Cinnamon teals (males on left and right). –JIM CLARK
Female cinnamon teal. –MARY TAYLOR GRAY

This mallard drake dwarfs the much smaller cinnamon teal (foreground). –MARY TAYLOR GRAY

Bald Eagle

Haliaeetus leucocephalus

A.K.A.: white-headed eagle, American eagle, Washington eagle

Family: Hawk

The bald eagle is a very large brown bird with a snowy white head and tail and yellow beak, legs, and feet. Immature birds are all brown with blotches of white on the tail and undersides. Immature bald eagles are often mistaken for golden eagles.

Natural History: The sight of a bald eagle truly quickens the heart and touches the viewer with a sense of awe, for these great birds of prey embody our image of wildness. Anyone who has seen a bald eagle in the wild is sure to mention the experience. It's not just their size that awes us, though they are the largest bird of prey in North America. The bald eagle's fierce look; strong, hooked bill; large, piercing talons; size; and strength and power add up to make it seem a natural symbol of our nation. Sadly, we allowed this magnificent bird to become endangered in the lower 48 states, and only intense recovery efforts and millions of dollars saved it from disappearing from the continental United States. In 1994 the bald eagle was downlisted from endangered to threatened status through all of its range except the extreme southwestern portion, in Arizona and part of New Mexico, where it remains endangered. This magnificent bird is now seen along rivers and lakes where it had previously been only a memory.

Roosting bald eagles have a particularly upright posture, unlike the forward lean of many hawks. It's not unusual to see a roost tree near water dotted with the white heads of these big eagles. Though we endow the bald eagle with all sorts of noble traits, its behavior is probably not particularly refined by human standards. Bald eagles are pirates, often robbing smaller raptors like ospreys and hawks of their hard-won prey. This larcenous habit caused Benjamin Franklin to consider the bald eagle "of bad moral character and not fit to become America's national bird." Bald eagles also eat carrion, a lowly habit by human standards, but a good way to ensure a meal. Eagles are primarily fish eaters. Their legs lack feathers, an adaptation to reduce drag in the water. Watch for them around open water, especially where there may be injured waterfowl. By contrast, golden eagles live in canyons and mountains and in nearby open country.

34

continued

Bald eagles develop their distinctive white head and tail plumage when they are four or five years old. –TERRY WYGANT

Bald Eagle
continued

Haliaeetus leucocephalus

When and Where to See Them: Around lakes, rivers, and open water in winter through most of Arizona, New Mexico, Utah, Colorado, and southeastern California.

Eyecatchers

The bald eagle's white head and great size, especially if you see one roosting in a tree, are a dead giveaway. In flight look for the white tail.

Roosting bald eagle. –JIM CLARK

Northern Harrier
Circus cyaneus

A.K.A.: marsh hawk

Family: Hawk

A slender-bodied hawk with long tail and tapered wings, the male is blue-gray with black wingtips and whitish underparts; the larger female is brown with streaked, whitish underparts. Both have a broad band of white at the base of the tail.

Natural History: You may know the harrier by its more familiar common name, marsh hawk. Many bird lovers objected to the official name change for this species because the old name so aptly described the lifestyle of this familiar wetlands raptor. In marshes and wetlands, even around irrigation canals along the edges of farm fields, the harrier flies just above the vegetation on wings tipped slightly up in a V, teetering a bit as if unsteady. The long tail with its broad white rump patch is an immediate identifier. Equipped with a dish-shaped ruff of feathers around the face that, similar to an owl's round face, helps gather sound, the harrier listens as well as looks for mice and other prey in the grass. Actually harrier is also a descriptive name for this bird that systematically searches a field, "harrying" its prey with short, swooping dives until the hunted bird or mouse flushes into the open.

Harrier courtship is a fascinating sight. In spring, the steel blue male flies high up in the air, then suddenly heels over and dives headfirst toward the ground. Pulling up and climbing high again, the male harrier dances a series of breathtaking U's in the air. The harrier female is brown and, as with many raptors, larger than her consort. During spring courtship the two may exchange food in midair, talon-to-talon, or drop food to each other, to be caught in the air.

When and Where to See Them: In wetlands, marshes, and open fields. Look for them year-round in Utah, Colorado, northern Arizona and New Mexico, and southern Nevada; late October through early April in southern Arizona, southern New Mexico, southeastern California, and far western Texas.

Eyecatchers

The harrier's low, teetering flight, with its wings tipped up in a V, is distinctive. Watch for the flash of the broad, white band at the base of the tail.

38

*Harriers typically fly low over marshland vegetation with their wings tipped up in a **V**.* –WENDY SHATTIL/BOB ROZINSKI

Female northern harriers have brown plumage and are larger than the blue-gray males. –WENDY SHATTIL/BOB ROZINSKI

Common Moorhen
Gallinula chloropus

A.K.A.: common gallinule,
blue peter, blue rail, water chicken

Family: Rail

This black water bird has a distinctive yellow-tipped red bill extending up the forehead, and very large yellow, chickenlike feet.

Natural History: Omigosh, those feet! The big feet of this "water chicken" let it sneak through marshy vegetation or walk atop floating vegetation looking for food. While most other members of the rail family are notoriously shy, the moorhen goes about its business heedless of human onlookers. You may see it pecking among plants on dry land, paddling about the water's surface, tipping "bottoms-up" like a duck to reach food just below the surface, diving after food, or even walking lightly on floating plants. Like its very common and widespread cousin, the **American coot**, the moorhen pumps its head forward and back as it swims. To help tell the difference between the two, look for the moorhen's red bill and forehead; the coot's bill is white. Moorhens are reluctant fliers, and watching them take off, it's no wonder. They flutter and splash across the surface with much wing flapping and running, only to drop back down into the marsh as soon as possible.

Moorhens build nests of rushes and cattails, suspended over water or partially floating, with a sloping runway of vegetation so the adults can come and go. Moorhens lay two and sometimes three clutches of eggs. In an odd quirk for the bird world, the young of the first brood perform a chore familiar to many older kids in human families—they help rear their younger brothers and sisters from later broods. They also help defend the family territory.

If you've ever listened to the cackles, squeaks, and squawks of coots and moorhens you know why they have nicknames like mudhen and water chicken.

When and Where to See Them: Year-round on marshes, ponds, and lakes with stands of cattails and reeds in central Arizona, New Mexico, far western Texas, and southeastern California.

Eyecatchers

This black, ducklike bird with a red bill pumps its head back and forth as it swims.

40

The common moorhen (above) has a red and yellow bill; the widely distributed American coot (below) has a white bill. –JIM CLARK

Note the moorhen's large feet. –MARY TAYLOR GRAY

Sandhill Crane
A.K.A.: brown crane, blue crane, turkey crane

Grus canadensis
Family: Crane

The sandhill is a four-foot-tall, gray bird with black wingtips, long sticklike legs, long neck and bill, and a naked red forehead.

Natural History: Even before first light on a winter morning at the Bosque del Apache National Wildlife Refuge south of Albuquerque, New Mexico, the indistinct shapes of large birds are discernible huddled along the water. As the light paints the sky smoky blue, then orange, the sandhill cranes sleeping in relative safety along the shallows begin to rustle and move. Here and there one leaps in the air, another flares its seven-foot wings, and a third bows then throws back its head. Soon cranes seem to fill the air as they move out in small groups to feed in the surrounding fields. Up to 20,000 sandhill cranes spend the winter in the area, moving south in fall along the Rocky Mountains from nesting grounds in northwestern Colorado, Wyoming, Idaho, and Montana. Amid the refuge's ponds and grain fields along the Rio Grande, built to provide habitat for waterfowl, the cranes find the shelter and food they need until it's time to return north in March.

In late afternoon the cranes begin to move back to the safety of the ponds, trailing in from all points of the compass, their eerie, trilling calls filling the air.

Cranes have wintered along the Rio Grande since long before European settlement, feeding on waste grain from the cornfields of the Pueblo peoples. A legend from the Picuris Pueblo tells how the cranes came to live along the Rio Grande. The cranes came down from the heavens (an explanation for their appearance after fall migration), drinking up all the water and eating all the food along many rivers. But when they came to the Rio Grande, they could not drink all the water and no matter how much they ate, there was still more. So, deciding this was a good and strong river, they made their home along it.

When and Where to See Them: The Bosque del Apache National Wildlife Refuge near Socorro, New Mexico, is the best place to see thousands of wintering sandhill cranes, from November

 continued

Sandhill cranes feed in fields and wet meadows **(above)** *by day, roosting at night in shallow water* **(below)** *where they are safer from predators.*

Sandhill Crane
continued

Grus canadensis

through early March. They are also visible in winter throughout the
southern half of the Southwest in farm fields with suitable nearby lakes
or ponds.

Eyecatchers

*The resonant call of the cranes—ka-rrooo, ka-rrooo—is like a
haunting voice of wildness. You can't mistake these large gray birds
feeding in grain fields or flying overhead like primordial creatures,
necks extended and legs held out behind.*

The flight profile of sandhill cranes is distinctive—long neck; long, outstretched legs; and large, undulating wings. –JIM CLARK

Killdeer
A.K.A.: killdee, meadow plover

Charadrius vociferus
Family: Plover

A boldly patterned shorebird, the killdeer has a reddish brown back, rump, and tail; white chest and belly; pink legs; and two dark neck rings.

Natural History: Screaming clamorously as it wheels and dives in the sky, cutting the air on tapered wings, or running tittering along the water's edge, like a turn-of-the-century bathing beauty with skirts lifted to expose skinny legs, the killdeer is nothing if not a showbird. Its best performance, though, is done in defense of its nest. When a predator, including a human, draws too near a killdeer's nest, the adult performs a "distraction display." The bird that a moment before had been shrieking lustily and dive-bombing the intruder suddenly appears wounded and vulnerable. Faking a broken wing, the adult staggers along in plain sight, dragging its wing, drawing the predator away from the nest. Then, as the predator moves in for an easy meal, the killdeer jumps into the air and is off with a screaming call.

Oddly, this devoted parent prepares a less than hospitable nest. The nest is at best a scrape in the ground or a collection of pebbles, sometimes in gravel parking lots or atop flat-roofed buildings. Killdeer young are able to leave the nest soon after hatching; you may see them pattering along after their mother. Killdeer feed on insects and other invertebrates found along the water's edge, in fields, and even on lawns.

When and Where to See Them: Year-round throughout the Southwest along lakes, rivers, streams and canals, meadows, and farm fields.

Eyecatchers

You can't mistake the killdeer's distinctive call—kill dee-dee-dee— and its scurry-and-stop running pattern. Watch as it repeatedly wheels and dives in flight, shrieking in a high-pitched voice, then swooping to skim low across the water.

46

Killdeer frequent the water's edge and open areas near water.

Belted Kingfisher
A.K.A.: halcyon, lazybird

Ceryle alcyon
Family: Kingfisher

The male belted kingfisher is a large-headed bird with a long, heavy bill; shaggy-topped blue head crest; blue-gray back; lighter breast and blue-gray breast band. The female has a rust-colored breast band below the blue one.

Natural History: If kingfishers are in the neighborhood, you'll hear their call—a chittering rattle. Kingfishers are always found near water, usually perching on a twig out over the water. They are easy to identify at a distance, their odd silhouette looking as if it were put together by committee—an oversized head with unkempt, cropped crest; almost no neck; seemingly no feet or legs; and a long, heavy bill. Their aggressive hunting style has earned these birds the title "king of the fishers." In characteristic kingfisher style, they swoop down from their twig perches to snag small fish from the water. Sometimes they hover in air above water, then drop down to grab prey.

In nesting season, the kingfisher pair digs a long tunnel in a streambank, sometimes as much as 15 feet long, with a chamber at the end to shelter their nest, usually little more than some twigs or a collection of grass. This burrow usually slopes up to prevent the accumulation of water. The constant arrival and departure of the adults carves two characteristic grooves at the burrow's entrance hole, worn by their dragging feet. As each adult returns to the nest, it sounds a call that is recognized by its mate. Kingfisher parents teach their young fishing skills by dropping bits of fish in the water for the juveniles to swoop down and retrieve.

When and Where to See Them: Along streams, rivers, canals, lakes, and ponds. Year-round in northern New Mexico; in winter and during migration in Arizona; southeastern California; southern Nevada, Utah, and New Mexico; and far western Texas.

Eyecatchers

You'll know the kingfisher by its posture and profile—blocky body with big head, long, thick bill, and above all, its punk-cut crest.

Watch for belted kingfishers perched on branches near or over water. –WENDY SHATTIL/BOB ROZINSKI

Black Phoebe

A.K.A.: black-headed flycatcher, western black pewee

Sayornis nigricans

Family: Tyrant flycatcher

The distinctive black body and head, with white belly and outer tail feathers, identify this phoebe, a small songbird with a rounded head and thin bill.

Natural History: Sycamores and other trees along canyon waterways are good places to see the handsome, sprightly little black phoebe. You'll probably hear its insistent *tsip* call and look up to find it perching in the branches above you, pumping its tail as it calls. The phoebe's song is no surprise—a bright *fee-bee*, with the second note lower than the first.

As their family name—flycatcher—implies, phoebes are insect eaters, sallying forth from a twig perch to snatch insects on the wing or on the ground. A phoebe often hunts just above the water surface where insects are abundant. You may hear the click of its bill as it snaps up a meal.

Phoebes are quite territorial, remaining on their "home turf" year-round. You may find their mud and grass nests glued beneath overhangs of buildings, bridges, or among the exposed roots of vegetation at the tops of cliffs and high banks above water. Their nests have even been found down old wells up to five feet deep.

When and Where to See Them: In trees and vegetation near water; in parks, canyons, valleys, and coastal plains. Year-round through much of the Southwest, moving into central and northern Arizona and New Mexico in summer.

Eyecatchers

The charming little phoebe appears dressed formally in black tails with a crisp white belly.

Black phoebe. —TOM J. ULRICH

Black phoebes build nests of mud and plant fibers along cliffs and under bridges or overhangs. —CHRIS GEANIOUS

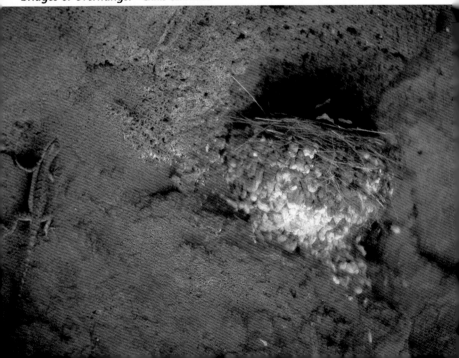

Vermilion Flycatcher

Pyrocephalus rubinus
Family: Tyrant flycatcher

The male flycatcher is dark brown with bright red head and underparts, brown eye mask, and a crest that can be raised or flattened. The female has a brown back, streaked breast, and salmon belly.

Natural History: What a show the male vermilion flycatcher puts on for his female during spring courtship. Rising from a mesquite tree or other perch, the male climbs upward, his red crest raised, breast feathers puffed out, and tail aloft. Singing a tinkling song, he hovers like a butterfly on rapidly beating wings, then flutters down in front of the object of his enthusiastic song flight. One hopes she is suitably impressed.

After mating, the pair selects a nest site in willows, cottonwoods, or mesquite trees near water. They build a sturdy nest of grass, plant fibers, spiderwebs, and other materials, set deep in the fork of a branch. The male feeds his mate as she sits on the eggs. He is a fearless defender of his nest.

Watch for vermilion flycatchers in the upper reaches of trees, where they seek their insect prey. They are known for catching bees in flight, and they sometimes land on the ground to go after grasshoppers. The flycatcher pumps its tail up and down as it perches.

The Spanish name for this flycatcher means "little cardinal"; the bird's Latin name—*pyrocephalus*—means "fire head," a good nickname for this showy little bird.

When and Where to See Them: In summer in streamside willows and trees or thickets along roadsides, often in the upper branches, in southeastern California, southwestern Utah, central to southern Arizona, southwestern New Mexico, and far western Texas. Year-round residents along the Mexican border.

Eyecatchers

A busy bit of bright red flits in the trees.

Vermilion flycatcher. –ROBERT E. BARBER

Red-winged Blackbird

Agelaius phoeniceus

A.K.A.: marsh blackbird; redwing

Family: Troupial

A glossy black bird with bold red wing patches edged in yellow, the red-winged blackbird is usually seen perched on a cattail. The female is a drab brown, lacks red on the wings, and blends well with marshland vegetation.

Natural History: Walk along a pond or marsh in spring and summer, or even a moist patch of ground that has sprouted a few cattails, and you'll likely be serenaded by the raucous song of red-winged blackbirds. The buzzing call of dozens of blackbirds, a bit like a discordant symphony of kazoos and triangles, fills the marsh with noise and life. *Konk-a-reeee* comes the call of one bird, soon echoed by another and another as each male announces dominion over his patch of turf—and beware to ye who enter here. Interlopers who trespass, whether fox, hawk, or human, may be dive-bombed and chased by male redwings seeking to drive them out. Redwings are very territorial birds. In spring the males arrive first at breeding areas, each claiming his patch of marshy territory among the cattails and vegetation. As the females arrive, the males sing and flash their bright red wing patches in a frenzy of spring courtship and territorial defense. In late summer and fall, after the young are on the wing, blackbirds gather in large flocks—the males in one group, the females and young in another—leaving the marsh by day to descend on meadows and grain fields to feed. Other blackbirds common in the Southwest include the **yellow-headed blackbird, Brewer's blackbird,** and **brown-headed cowbird.**

Notice how the scarlet wing patch is visible on some males, but not on others? The birds can either expose the patch or cover it with wing feathers. Why? Studies of these "badges" show they are important symbols of status within the redwing community. Males who enter another's territory cover their badges to be less conspicuous. If they don't, they are liable to be aggressively attacked. If no one attacks, the intruder soon uncovers his red wing patches and starts defending the new territory as his own. On the other hand, males whose red badges were painted black by researchers had a hard time defending their territories—apparently, badge-less males must appear less threatening to other males.

continued

Red-winged blackbirds are among the most familiar—and noisy—marshland songbirds. –BRYAN H. PRIDGEON

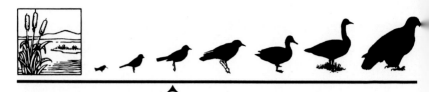

Red-winged Blackbird

Agelaius phoeniceus

continued

When and Where to See Them: Year-round among thick
vegetation around freshwater marshes, flooded fields, and riparian areas.

Eyecatchers

> *You can't miss the bright scarlet wing patches on this handsome,
> coal black bird. The male's loud, buzzing call may announce the
> redwing before you actually see him.*

Red-winged blackbird. –JIM CLARK

Summer Tanager
A.K.A.: bee bird, redbird, calico warbler

Pirangra rubra

Family: Tanager

This bright rosy red bird is the color of a cardinal, but lacks a crest. The female has a golden breast and undersides with an olive back and wings.

Natural History: The male summer tanager sings a rich, whistling melody, the notes rising and falling similar to a robin's, but with a faster tempo. The summer tanager is nicknamed bee bird because it seems to consider bees and wasps to be special treats. Beekeepers report that tanagers sometimes haunt an apiary, plucking the industrious bees from the air as they come and go. Tanagers are also known to tear into wasps' nests seeking the tender larvae. Tanagers eat a variety of other insects and become quite tame in some gardens, where they are definitely a gardener's friend, eating the larvae and adults of all kinds of insects. Tanagers spend much of their time amid the upper branches of trees where the insects are, so when looking for tanagers, look toward the treetops.

Summer tanagers are southerners, summer residents not only of the Southwest but also of the Dixie states, their range extending into the southern fringes of the Midwest. The **hepatic tanager** is about the same size as the summer, but a duller red. It lives at higher elevations amid mountain forests of pine and oak. The brightly colored **western tanager,** with yellow body, black wings, and red head, is a summer resident of mountain coniferous forests of the West from the Mexican border to the Northwest Territories of Canada.

When and Where to See Them: In summer throughout the Southwest at low elevations in canyons, and along streams amid willows and cottonwood groves.

Eyecatchers

Like a bright red tree ornament, the summer tanager adorns cottonwood and willow thickets along streams and canyons of the Southwest.

Summer tanager. –MARY TAYLOR GRAY

BIRDS OF OPEN COUNTRY

▼▼▼▼▼▼▼▼▼▼▼▼

Deserts, Grasslands, and Shrublands

Turkey vulture
Red-tailed hawk
American kestrel
Scaled quail
Gambel's quail
Inca dove
Mourning dove
Greater roadrunner
Great horned owl
Elf owl
Burrowing owl
Lesser nighthawk
Common poorwill
Black-chinned hummingbird
Costa's hummingbird
Gila woodpecker

Western kingbird
Horned lark
Cactus wren
Northern mockingbird
Curve-billed thrasher
Phainopepla
Loggerhead shrike
Northern cardinal
Pyrrhuloxia
Blue grosbeak
Black-throated sparrow
White-crowned sparrow
Western meadowlark
Great-tailed grackle
Hooded oriole
House finch

Turkey Vulture

A.K.A.: turkey buzzard, carrion crow, John crow

Cathartes aura
Family: American vulture

Usually seen soaring high in the air, the turkey vulture is a large, black bird with naked, red head, curved bill, and six-foot wing span.

Natural History: Vultures are as familiar a sight in western movies as John Wayne. There they are, circling in the air above the spot where Indians have attacked, or waiting for some hapless desert wanderer to die. It's a trite, B-western cliché: vulture equals bad stuff. But while American western culture reviles them as foul creatures and harbingers of doom, the vulture and its kin, the California condor, are revered by some Native Americans who believe the dead are carried to the heavens by these high-soaring birds.

You may cringe at the thought of a turkey vulture, but these scavenging carrion eaters perform a vital natural function, helping to "recycle" dead animals. The Pueblo peoples considered the vulture a powerful medicine man associated with purification and cleansing. In this century vultures have suffered at human hands by feeding on poisoned carcasses set out to kill coyotes and other predators. They've benefited, though, from a new human-supplied food source—roadkill.

Affably referred to as TV's by birdwatchers, turkey vultures are wonderfully designed for scavenging carrion in open country. A vulture's eyesight is so acute it can spot an animal carcass on the ground while soaring as high as two and a half miles (some experts claim four miles), distances at which a human can't even see a bird in the sky. Its naked head lacks feathers, making it much easier to clean, an important feature, considering what the vulture is sticking its head into when feeding. Once high in the air, vultures seldom flap their wings, staying aloft by soaring on thermals—rising columns of warm air. Though it glides downward, the vulture falls at a slower rate than the air rises. The design of the vulture's wing allows it to stay aloft at slow speed without stalling. Its five-foot wing span gives the bird a high surface-to-weight ratio. Watching these birds spiraling higher in the sky till they disappear in the heavens, you'll understand why some Indian tribes thought them messengers of the gods.

continued

Turkey vulture. –TERRY WYGANT

Red-tailed Hawk
A.K.A.: redtail, hen hawk

Buteo jamaicensis
Family: Hawk

Both sexes of this large brown hawk have a pale, streaked breast, dark belly band, and a tail that is rusty red above. Wings are broad and rounded. Two other color phases—an almost solid dark brown, and a pale form with a head and tail that are almost white—make identification confusing, but these forms are not common in the Southwest.

Natural History: You've heard it a million times on TV, the chilling *Keeeer!* scream of the red-tailed hawk, arcing downward in pitch like a rock tossed off a cliff. It's a perfect way to set the scene for someplace wild and western. The familiar redtail is the most common and widespread hawk in North America, its abundance leading to a birdwatcher's adage for identifying hawks—"If all else fails, call it a redtail." Whether you see it circling lazily in the air, surveying its hunting grounds from atop a telephone pole, or swooping down to pounce upon a rabbit or mouse, the sight of a redtail is somehow reassuring—proof that there are still places wild enough for a hawk to exist.

Morning is a great time to see these stout-bodied, broad-winged hawks as they flap slowly upward in the cool, early morning air. As the sun warms the sky, rising columns of air called thermals carry the hawks to vantage points high in the sky. Here they circle on outstretched wings, carving slow arcs against an endless blue sky.

Redtail courtship can be a stunning spectacle as the pair spirals about each other in air, screaming and performing amazing acrobatic feats. The smaller male sometimes drops down toward the female from high above her. She turns on her back and they touch or grasp talons in mock combat. Once mated, the pair stays together for life, or until one dies, when the survivor chooses a new mate. A mated pair returns to nest in the same territory year after year. They build a bulky platform nest of sticks (which may be usurped by early nesting great horned owls) that they defend by screaming and diving at intruders.

When and Where to See Them: Year-round throughout the Southwest in open country, shrublands, deserts, and mountains.

continued

4-29-00

Verde
River
Canyon

Seeking high vantage points when they hunt, red-tailed hawks commonly perch on human-made structures, such as power poles.

Red-tailed Hawk
continued

Buteo jamaicensis

Eyecatchers
▽ ▽ ▽ ▽ ▽ ▽ ▽

The reddish tail of this large brown hawk is very noticeable in the right light. The redtail's size, four-foot wing span, and piercing scream help identify it.

The red-tailed hawk can often be identified by its red tail. −MARY TAYLOR GRAY

American Kestrel

A.K.A.: sparrow hawk,
grasshopper hawk, mouse hawk

Falco sparverius
Family: Falcon

A striking, robin-sized falcon, the male has blue-gray wings, rusty red back with black barring, a peach-colored breast, and a rufous-red tail. The crown of the head is blue-gray with a reddish spot. The female is similar to the male but her wings are brown, not blue. Both sexes have two vertical black streaks, called "whiskers," on each cheek.

Natural History: Ever notice a small bird hovering almost upright on rapidly beating wings, tail spread to hold position, and eyes scanning the ground? You've seen a kestrel in action.

The smallest of North American raptors (excluding owls), the kestrel is also among the most common and one that has adapted well to life around humans. You've probably driven past kestrels hundreds of times, not realizing that what looked like just another songbird perched on a wire or in a tree was actually a fierce hunter. This small, handsome falcon is a treat to watch. Although larger hawks hunt from the air or perch on a vantage point, the kestrel typically hovers over open ground, scanning the grass below for possible prey. Nicknamed sparrow hawks because they were once flown at sparrows by falconers, kestrels feed mainly on grasshoppers, as well as on mice and, in winter, small birds. The kestrel's sleek, tapering wings and long tail make it a fleet and maneuverable flier, but unlike most falcons, it tends to drop upon prey on the ground rather than grab it in the air.

The kestrel's call is a distinctive *killy-killy-killy*. Kestrels nest in old woodpecker holes and nooks and crannies in barns and buildings. When the hunting male returns home, he calls the female from the nest to feed her. He may even sit on the eggs, an unusual habit among birds of prey.

When and Where to See Them: Year-round throughout the Southwest in deserts, grasslands, open woodlands, shrublands, and in and around cities.

Eyecatchers

Look for a small bird with pointed wings, peachy breast, and red and gunmetal blue coloring, hovering over open land or perched on a power line. Up close, the facial "whiskers" are unmistakable.

Male American kestrel. –WENDY SHATTIL/BOB ROZINSKI

Scaled Quail
A.K.A.: cottontop, blue quail,
topknot quail

Callipepla squamata
Family: Pheasant

Scaly markings on its breast and back and a triangular, white-tipped head crest identify this pale, grayish quail.

Natural History: The scaled quail seems to wear an expression of perpetual surprise. With a feathery crest spiking up from its head it looks like a cartoon character who has just been startled. The white tip of this crest can be spotted at a distance, hence the bird's nickname cottontop. So well does it match its surroundings, its name in the Tewa Indian language means "sagebrush softness."

Quails are social birds, living together much of the year in groups called coveys, which may number from 7 to 150 birds. The covey breaks up for nesting; after the young leave the nest, family groups of adults and puffball chicks are often seen scurrying about beneath vegetation. As his family forages, the male acts as sentinel, watching for danger from a vantage point. These endearing little quails are desert dwellers, inhabiting a land of mesquite, creosote, and cactus. But they have learned to take advantage of the resources found near humans and are frequent visitors around ranches, feeding on livestock grain and drinking from stock tanks. Their call is a nasal *pe-COS*.

A true desert dweller, the scaled quail's life cycle depends on rain. It nests in early summer when the rains bring forth tender new growth, lots of insects, and water puddles for chicks to drink from. In very dry years, scaled quails may not nest at all, waiting until the next year to better the chances of survival for their young.

When and Where to See Them: Year-round in high desert, shrublands, valleys, on low mesas, and at canyon mouths, often near water.

Eyecatchers
▼▼▼▼▼▼▼▼

A spiky crest of feathers bristles from its head.

72

The scaled quail is named for the scaly appearance of its plumage. −ROBERT E. BARBER

Gambel's Quail
A.K.A.: Arizona quail, desert quail

Callipepla gambelii
Family: Pheasant

This plump gray quail has reddish brown sides streaked with white and a characteristic head feather arching up from the forehead. The male has a reddish cap, black face and throat, with white lines down the cheeks and across the forehead and a black spot on the belly.

Natural History: The Gambel's quail looks like nothing so much as a tiny, avian sultan, the upright plume of its "turban" bobbing as it moves about the desert floor in a courtly fashion.

Quail belong to a family of chickenlike birds that includes pheasants, ptarmigan, partridge and the ancestors of domestic chickens. They spend most of their time on the ground, not a bad choice in a land lacking in large trees. Quail are well known to hunters for sitting motionless on the ground until the very last second, bursting suddenly from cover when practically underfoot. Desert visitors are soon entranced by the milling coveys of quail foraging beneath desert vegetation, scurrying out of reach if a human approaches too closely. Gambel's quail have been clocked on the ground at faster than 15 mph. After the chicks hatch, the family leaves the nest, traveling (on foot, of course) in formation—father in the lead, puffball chicks in the middle, mother bringing up the rear. In fall extended families gather together in large coveys, roosting in shrubs at night. When the morning dawns, the birds jump to the ground, visit the communal drinking hole, then move out to forage for the day. Their chuckling, grunting calls bubble out as the covey moves, matching their milling, bobbing manner of walking. If a bird becomes separated from its compadres, it sounds a loud, high-pitched location call—*chi-CA-go-go*—that has an almost questioning quality, as if to say, "Where are you guys?"

When and Where to See Them: Year-round in low deserts and shrublands, usually near water; throughout southern Arizona, southern New Mexico, the deserts of California, and in far western Texas.

Eyecatchers

The upright plume, looping up from the head like a comma on end, and the male's color and head markings are striking.

Roosting Inca doves. –STEVE RENZI

Inca dove and young. –SHIRLEY BERQUIST

Mourning Dove
A.K.A.: turtle dove, wood dove

Zenaida macroura
Family: Pigeon

This pigeonlike bird has iridescent, gray-brown plumage, dark wing spots, small head, slender neck, and buffy underparts. The long, spade-shaped tail has white edges, and is very noticeable in flight.

Natural History: The gentle mourning dove is a familiar friend, whether striding about the ground, its small head bobbing back and forth with each step, or perched in our backyards, parks, golf courses—practically anywhere we turn. In flight the mourning dove's small head, long tail, and stubby wings form a stylized cross. The soft, sad cooing that gives the dove its name provides sweet music, punctuated by the whistling of its wing feathers as it flies up to roost.

In keeping with their gentle manner, mourning doves, which mate for life, seem affectionate pairs to human watchers. The two sit side by side, the male cooing softly, the female answering quietly. With closed eyes these "lovebirds" bow their heads, lean against each other, and rub necks, a true display of the term "billing and cooing."

Weed and grass seeds make up 98 percent of a dove's diet. Like other ground birds, they swallow grit to help grind these hard foods in their gizzard, a muscular part of the stomach. Mourning doves live in diverse habitats in the arid Southwest—mesquite deserts, farmlands, towns and suburbs, grasslands, mountains—and sometimes fly long distances to find water. The **white-winged dove** looks similar to the mourning dove, but is much more limited in its range, inhabiting deserts and shrublands of southern Arizona. It is gray-brown with large, white wing and tail patches and a rounded tail.

When and Where to See Them: Year-round throughout the Southwest in shrublands, open woodlands, backyards, parks, and mountains up to timberline.

Eyecatchers
▼▼▼▼▼▼▼

The dove's head-bobbing walk and small-headed, plump-bodied shape are distinctive. Listen for its whistling wings and its sad, mournful cooing. Watch for the white edges of its spade-shaped tail in flight.

78

Mourning dove. —MARY TAYLOR GRAY

White-winged dove. —PAUL BERQUIST

Greater Roadrunner   *Geococcyx californianus*
A.K.A.: correo del camino, lizard bird,   **Family: Cuckoo**
paisano (countryman)

A large ground bird streaked and flecked with brown; white underparts; large head with shaggy crest; very long tail with white-tipped outer feathers; long, heavy bill; and long blue legs identify the roadrunner.

Natural History: A fascinating, curious bird, and one of the symbols of the Southwest, the roadrunner is a treat to see, the kind of sighting you tell friends about.

The roadrunner inspired respect, admiration, and a sense of compatriotism among Native Americans and Hispanics, who knew well this courageous, hardy hunter of the desert. Its nicknames are many—snake killer, lizard bird, even paisano, or countryman. Certainly southwestern people felt a kinship with this bird that could survive in the harsh and beautiful landscape they also called home. The roadrunner figures in the legends of some southwestern Indian tribes for its skill, ingenuity, and courage in killing rattlesnakes; it is reputed to corral snakes within a circle of cactus spines. While the cartoon roadrunner may seem like a lucky near-victim of Wile E. Coyote, the real-life roadrunner is no dupe. In addition to eating any insects and lizards it can find, this plucky bird eats the fruits of cactus and catches scorpions, tarantulas, and snakes, including rattlesnakes.

The roadrunner is beautifully adapted to desert life. In winter, it uses solar energy to stay warm, turning its back to the sun, extending its wings and raising the feathers on its back to expose its black, heat-absorbing skin. In the brutal desert heat, roadrunners seek shade in the hottest part of the day, compressing their feathers so they will not trap heat. By fluttering the skin on the throat to force air across the respiratory membranes, they make use of evaporative cooling. With a curious arrangement of the toes—two pointing forward, and two facing back—the roadrunner leaves an X footprint in the sand.

Roadrunners form a lifelong pair bond; they also maintain their territory throughout the year. The male does most of the incubating. Eggs within a clutch hatch at different times; in a year of limited resources, the youngest chicks will starve and be eaten by their parents and sib-

80

continued

Greater roadrunner. –MARY TAYLOR GRAY

Greater Roadrunner *Geococcyx californianus*
continued

lings. This may seem harsh to humans, but it is a strategy to maximize resources and the chances for survival of the strongest individuals. Three weeks after hatching, the young roadrunners are catching their own dinners.

When and Where to See Them: Year-round in Arizona, New Mexico, and Texas, southeastern California, southern Nevada, and southwestern Utah, in desert and mesquite and chaparral shrublands.

Eyecatchers

Watch for a large, long-tailed bird running or walking on the ground, everything about it implying speed.

In cold weather, the greater roadrunner takes advantage of solar heating by exposing its dark under-plumage and skin to the sun. –MARY TAYLOR GRAY

Great Horned Owl
A.K.A.: hoot owl, cat owl

Bubo virginianus
Family: Owl

This large, stocky owl has big yellow eyes, white throat, and two feathery "horns" on the head. Plumage is brown with black barring. Gold disks formed of feathers frame the face.

Natural History: Nothing sets the stage so well for an evening in the woods than the eerie hooting of a great horned owl. Often a second owl will answer the first, and the two will set up a call-and-response duet that can go on for hours. Don't spend too much time trying to locate the callers, though, because these birds are great ventriloquists, and you'd have a hard time seeing them at night anyway. The owl is more likely to find you, sweeping suddenly by on wings so silent you won't know the bird is there until you feel its passage. The owl's wing feathers have serrated edges that allow air to slip past without creating vibration, hence their nearly soundless flight. Because they are creatures of the night, owls have been thought by many cultures to possess supernatural powers. Though it's unlikely they really foresee events, their powers certainly are supernatural compared with human abilities. Their large, forward-facing eyes are the same size as a human's, but their vision is 100 times more acute. The feathered disk around the face increases the amount of light gathered by the eyes, helping the bird see in what we would perceive as total darkness. But it is the owl's hearing ability that is truly amazing. The feathered facial disk also acts as a giant ear, capturing sound as well as light. An owl's hearing is so acute it can pinpoint a mouse's location in near darkness merely from the rodent's rustling and squeaks. One of the owl's ears is set higher than the other. By moving its head to equalize sound, the owl aligns the source of the sound with its line of vision. A little squeak, a little scurry, and the mouse is done in by an ear with talons.

The great horned owl is the most common and widespread owl in North America. Its barred, gray-brown plumage is such good camouflage you've probably passed by one roosting above you without ever seeing it. Owls are one of the most important predators of rodents and rabbits; they also prey on skunks, porcupines, and other birds. The great horned is such a fierce and voracious predator it has been dubbed "winged tiger."

continued

Great horned owl. –TERRY WYGANT

Great Horned Owl
continued

Bubo virginianus

When and Where to See Them: Throughout the Southwest in deserts, woodlands, mountains, canyons, near water, and in cities and suburbs.

Eyecatchers

A large, blocky shape roosts on a tree limb near the trunk, sporting two feathery horns that blow gently in the breeze. At night, a large silent shape sweeps suddenly past you. You'll instantly recognize its resonant hooting, a characteristic hoo oo oo.

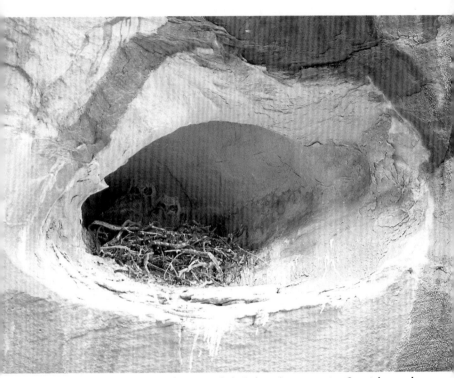

Great horned owlets await the return of their hunting parents. Great horned owls are early nesters that usually use the old nests of hawks, crows, ravens, or other birds. –TERRY WYGANT

Elf Owl
A.K.A.: Whitney's owl

Micrathene whitneyi
Family: Owl

Mottled brown plumage with buffy underparts, round head lacking ear tufts, yellow eyes, and short tail identify this sparrow-sized owl.

Natural History: The desert holds many delights, among them the sight of an elf owl peering wide-eyed from its hole in a saguaro cactus. Elf is an appropriate name for this little owl, the smallest in the world. Measuring only five to six inches in length, the owl is smaller than many songbirds. The elf owl is the most common owl in Arizona and remains fairly abundant there in canyons and deserts, though it is nearly gone from Texas; efforts have been made to reintroduce it to the California desert. Elf owls are not only tiny, they're also nocturnal. Though many desert visitors will probably never see one, they may hear them. At dusk, as they emerge from their daytime roost holes, they whistle and chuckle. Their yiplike calls have been likened to the cries of a puppy and are surprisingly loud.

Considering their diminutive stature, these owls are unlikely to carry off cottontails like their cousin the great horned. Elf owls hunt prey more their size—insects—though the owls aren't much larger than some of the big moths they catch. Elf owls use several hunting techniques—they grab flying insects from the air with their talons like a falcon; sally forth from a perch to snag a meal in the air like a flycatcher; and hover around flowers like hummingbirds, though their quarry is flower-feeding insects, not nectar. Elf owls even catch scorpions, snapping off the creature's stinger, then swallowing the rest. In canyons and foothills, elf owls are found amid stands of oak and sycamore.

When and Where to See Them: In low deserts, canyons, and foothills of Arizona and southwestern New Mexico. They are few in number in far western Texas and southeastern California.

Eyecatchers

Look for an owl face peering at you from a hole in a saguaro cactus, or listen for this tiny owl's loud, yipping call, heard at dusk.

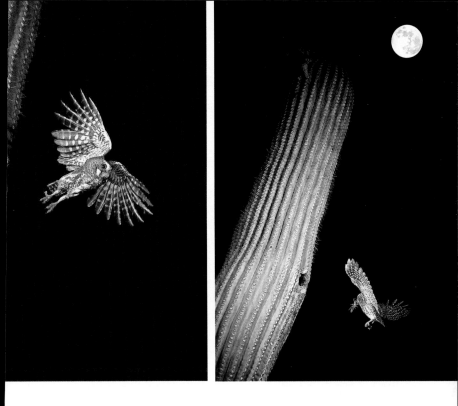

Elf owls nest in holes originally excavated by woodpeckers in saguaro cactus.
—PAUL AND SHIRLEY BERQUIST

Burrowing Owl

Speotyto cunicularia

A.K.A.: Ground owl, billy owl, howdy owl

Family: Owl

This small brown owl is flecked with white, with long legs, round yellow eyes, white neck collar, and barred breast. Watch for it on the ground or flying within a prairie dog town. At a distance it appears about the size and shape of a prairie dog.

Natural History: Look closely at the round-headed shapes sitting on prairie dog mounds in spring and summer and you may be surprised to realize some of them are long-legged, ground-dwelling owls.

Despite their name, burrowing owls don't actually dig into the ground. They use the abandoned tunnels of prairie dogs, ground squirrels, kangaroo rats, and other burrowing rodents. Burrowing owls nest in the same colony year after year as long as they are not disturbed. If there is too much human activity around the site, they won't return. Some historic nesting sites have been abandoned once encircled by development.

Burrowing owl courtship is rather touching to human observers. The pair "bill and coo," calling softly to each other and rubbing their necks and bills together. They also bob and bow comically. Both adults incubate the eggs. By midsummer, the young owls crowd about the burrow entrance in a cluster of round heads and big yellow eyes. When disturbed, the young make a noise that sounds like a rattlesnake, an attempt to scare away predators.

Burrowing owls feed mainly on insects and small rodents. They and their prairie dog hosts are usually tolerant neighbors. The owls are too small to be a serious threat to prairie dogs, which outweigh the birds significantly. But occasionally the owls take a young prairie dog and the dogs in turn sometimes eat an unguarded owl egg.

Prairie dogs are important hosts to burrowing owls over much of the birds' range. As prairie dog populations have declined (an estimated 90 to 95 percent from presettlement times) due to agricultural and urban development and extensive eradication efforts, so have the numbers of the ground-dwelling owls that depend on these burrowing rodents. Biologists fear this curious owl, so well adapted to life in open country, may be in serious trouble.

continued

Burrowing owl and young. –JAN L. WASSINK

Burrowing Owl
continued

Speotyto cunicularia

When and Where to See Them: Throughout the Southwest spring through fall; year-round in the southern part of the region; in prairies, deserts, old fields, and other open ground, particularly in prairie dog towns. Look for them on top of burrow mounds and on nearby fence posts and high points.

Eyecatchers

These little brown owls sit atop the mounds of a prairie dog town or fly low through the dog town, often from one mound to another.

Burrowing owls commonly perch on low vantage points near their nest burrows. −BRYAN H. PRIDGEON

Lesser Nighthawk

A.K.A.: trilling nighthawk

Chordeiles acutipennis

Family: Nightjar

This well-camouflaged bird is mottled and barred with brown, gray, and white, with white bands around the tail and a white or buffy throat. White wing bars are noticeable in flight. The head is very round, with a short bill.

Natural History: Like all nightjars, the lesser nighthawk has a gaping, "catcher's mitt" mouth, the better to engulf flying insects. The lesser nighthawk resembles its more widespread cousin, the **common nighthawk**. Though the lesser is slightly smaller (that makes sense), both have long, tapering wings with distinctive white wing bars, white throats, and white bars on the tail. The lesser hunts lower to the ground and has a fluttering style of flight. You can avoid confusing the two by remembering the lesser nighthawk is a bird of the lowlands, while the common nighthawk, in the Southwest at least, is mainly a high country bird. Listen for the lesser's distinctive soft trilling or whirring call, which has been likened to the singing of a toad. Trying to locate the bird by its call will convince you the lesser nighthawk is an accomplished ventriloquist.

As its name implies, the lesser nighthawk is abroad at dusk and night, though it is sometimes active until much later in the morning than other nightjars. The lesser nighthawk can go into a shallow resting state, called torpor, when food is scarce or temperatures cold. This allows the bird to conserve energy.

When and Where to See Them: In southern New Mexico, southwestern Texas, eastern California, and most of Arizona; in dry, open, low-elevation shrublands and deserts from April to October.

Eyecatchers

The nighthawk has white wing bars and a trilling call.

Lesser nighthawk. –BRYAN H. PRIDGEON

Common Poorwill

A.K.A.: dusky poorwill

Phalaenoptilus nuttallii
Family: Nightjar

A round-headed, short-tailed, very well-camouflaged bird, the poorwill is speckled brown, gray, and white, with a white collar and very large eyes.

Natural History: You aren't likely to see the poorwill, but you have a good chance of hearing its *poor-will* call if you're out in the desert at night. Like others of their family, poorwills rest by day, their mottled plumage providing ideal camouflage against a backdrop of desert rocks, soil, and vegetation. In evening they venture abroad to hunt, fluttering around like giant moths snapping up insects in their wide mouths or springing from the ground to grab a passing meal, then settling back to the same spot. If you do see a poorwill, it will likely be a quick glimpse of a low-flying bird or one perched on the highway, its eyes glowing pink in the shine of your headlights. Don't get this bird confused with its larger, more familiar cousin, the **whip-poor-will**, known for its *whip-poor-will* call repeated over and over between dusk and dawn. Though mainly a species of eastern woodlands, the whip-poor-will does inhabit densely wooded canyons and mountains of the Southwest.

Ever hear of a bird hibernating? Well, that's what the poorwill does. Swifts and some other birds enter a shallow dormant state, but the common poorwill is the only bird known to hibernate, reducing its temperature, breathing, and heart rate and falling into a deep sleep. Though this ability was only discovered by the scientific community in the 1940s, the Hopi Indians knew the poorwill by the name *holchko* meaning "the sleeping one."

When and Where to See Them: Throughout the Southwest in desert and open shrub and grasslands; at evening and night, mainly from April through September, with only a slight chance in the colder months.

Eyecatchers

The haunting poor-will *call echoes out of the desert night.*

—CHRIS GEANIOUS

The common poorwill's camouflaging plumage allows it to blend into its habitat of rock, earth, and dry vegetation.

—D. AND M. ZIMMERMAN/VIREO

Black-chinned Hummingbird

A.K.A.: black-chin

Archilochus alexandri

Family: Hummingbird

A medium-sized hummingbird, the male is iridescent green with a black throat and white collar below it. A purple patch on his lower throat flashes in the right light. The female is green with white underparts.

Natural History: Flowers are the key for attracting humming-birds. After a winter in Mexico, these buzzing bundles of avian energy head north, funneling up through the flowering deserts and fertile canyons of Arizona across the Southwest to nest as far north as Montana and southern British Columbia. They feed on nectar-producing flowers such as paloverde, chuparosa, and scarlet larkspur, and are attracted to the flowers by color. That's why hummers sometimes buzz very close to us when we're wearing brightly colored clothes. Some hummers also drink sap from the sap wells drilled by sapsuckers (a group of woodpeckers). Native Americans of the Southwest associated these brilliantly colored birds with the rainbow and considered them messengers of the rain spirits.

Male hummingbirds perform elaborate courtship flights in spring, each species with a characteristic flight pattern. The black-chin flies back and forth like a buzzing pendulum in front of the object of his interest, winging up 15 feet in the air, then zooming down and up again in an arc, his wings whirring like a bee. The hummer's tiny cone-shaped nest—maybe an inch high and an inch and a half across—is made of plant down and covered with the silk from spiderwebs. Placed in the fork of a branch, usually near or over water, it holds two tiny, half-inch white eggs.

The black-chin is closely related to—more or less the western version of—the widespread ruby-throated hummingbird of the East and Midwest.

When and Where to See Them: Throughout the Southwest from late March through late August in wooded canyons, valleys, deserts, mountain meadows, urban gardens, and at hummingbird feeders.

Eyecatchers

The black throat, which flashes magenta in the light, is edged by a broad white band on this metallic green hummer.

98

Male black-chinned hummingbird. –WENDY SHATTIL/BOB ROZINSKI

Costa's Hummingbird

A.K.A.: hummer

Calypte costae

Family: Hummingbird

The male is iridescent, metallic green with whitish underparts. Its head and gorget of throat feathers, which it flares out in a long tusk on each side, appear black until caught in the right light, when they shimmer to purple. The female is green above with dull white underparts (and impossible to tell from the female black-chinned hummer).

Natural History: If you've made the mistake of consigning hummingbirds to the ranks of the insignificant just because they're small, you haven't experienced a male hummer during breeding season. Just watch the male Costa's hummingbird. He looks like a dark-headed, green-bodied generic hummingbird, until he turns his head. Catching the light just right, his head and neck flash a gorgeous, deep reddish purple. This isn't just a casual accident of the light. It's a deliberate display by the tiny bird. And as he displays, he flares out his gorget, a collar of feathers projecting from his throat like the drooping ends of an enormous handlebar mustache. It's a bit like the hummingbird version of bicep-flexing. Add his spectacular, buzzing courtship flight—a dazzling display of loops and dives, repeated over and over from favorite perch to favorite perch—and the tiny hummer can be as territorial and aggressive as any male.

The larger **broad-tailed hummingbird,** the common hummer of the Rocky Mountains, with green back and ruby throat, nests in mountain forests and meadows of the Southwest. The **Anna's hummingbird** lives year-round in the southwestern corner of Arizona and the California deserts.

When and Where to See Them: In deserts and low shrublands of southern Arizona and southeastern California from March through July.

Eyecatchers

The amazing throat gorget of feathers, which flare out from the sides of the neck like the long whiskers of an old man, appear black until they catch the light, flashing a dazzling magenta-purple.

The mustachelike, iridescent gorget of the male Costa's hummingbird becomes noticeable when it catches the light. —TOM J. ULRICH

Male broad-tailed hummingbird . —WENDY SHATTIL/BOB ROZINSKI

Male Anna's hummingbird. —MARY TAYLOR GRAY

Gila Woodpecker

A.K.A.: saguaro woodpecker

Melanerpes uropygialis

Family: Woodpecker

This large woodpecker sports black and white striping on the back and tail, gray head, neck, and belly. The male has a bright red cap.

Natural History: If you've visited the deserts of Arizona, especially the Sonoran Desert with its giant saguaro cactus, you've seen gila woodpeckers (if not, you had your eyes closed). Named after the Gila River (pronounced HEE-la) where they were first seen by Europeans, these large, zebra-striped woodpeckers with the red caps can't be missed as they perch conspicuously on the sides of saguaro or other desert vegetation. They are the principal architects (along with gilded flickers) of the many picturesque holes in saguaro, which provide vital nesting cavities not for just woodpeckers but for many other animals including elf owls, phainopeplas, house finches, rats, mice, snakes, and lizards.

Gila woodpeckers eat a diverse diet, a wise strategy in a sometimes hostile desert environment where one must make use of all available resources. They consume a great many insects, the fruits of cactus (especially saguaro), mistletoe berries, acorns, the eggs of other birds, and the fleshy pulp of cactus.

Be careful not to confuse the Gila woodpecker with the smaller **ladder-backed woodpecker,** which is zebra-striped but has a larger red cap, a red nape, and horizontal stripes on the face; or the **gilded flicker,** with a brown and white back, red cheek patches, black half-moon on the chest, and yellow wing feathers visible in flight.

When and Where to See Them: Year-round in saguaro desert, dry washes, shrublands, woodlands, and cottonwood groves along rivers, and occasionally in canyons to about 4,000 feet. In southeastern California, southwestern New Mexico, the tip of Nevada, and central and southern Arizona.

Eyecatchers

Watch for the flashing white wing patches when the bird flies and the bird's zebra-striping and red cap.

Gila woodpecker.

Western Kingbird

A.K.A.: Arkansas kingbird

Tyrannus verticalis

Family: Tyrant flycatcher

Look for a gray bird with sulfur yellow belly and darker wings and tail. The outer edges of the tail are white.

Natural History: Watch a western kingbird for a while and you'll observe the hunting style typical of the tyrant flycatchers. Kingbirds wait on an exposed perch for an insect to fly by, then dart out, grab it in air, and loop back to the same perch to repeat the process. Sometimes you can hear the click of their bills as they snap up their prey.

Tyrant flycatchers are named not just for their hunting method but also for their aggressiveness. Watch them in defense of their home territories and you'll see why the kingbird's common name is apt; they are definitely the "king birds" of their world. Kingbirds will pursue and dive-bomb trespassers, even riding on the backs of hawks so rude as to venture above the kingbird's turf. By contrast, they are sociable with those of their own species, several pairs sometimes nesting in the same tree. Groups of kingbirds will also band together to mob hawks, crows, and ravens that come near their nests.

Nearly as synonymous with grasslands as meadowlarks, western kingbirds seem to occupy every fence wire and post across a piece of rangeland. Fields, roadsides, and shrublands are good kingbird habitat because of the abundance of flying insects. Adult kingbirds are dutiful parents, teaching their young to hunt by trapping insects and releasing them for the young to catch. In the Southwest, another very similar kingbird—**Cassin's kingbird**—inhabits higher-elevation forests of sycamore and conifer, as well as some of the same habitat as the western.

When and Where to See Them: From April through September, perched on wire fences and in trees along roadsides and fields throughout the Southwest.

Eyecatchers

These gray-and-yellow birds are often seen perched on a wire or twig tip. They will mob and drive off magpies and hawks (and humans) in aggressive defense of their nests.

Western kingbird. –WENDY SHATTIL/BOB ROZINSKI

Horned Lark

Eremophila alpestris

A.K.A.: snow lark

Family: Lark

This gray-brown bird has a white breast, yellow throat, black chest collar, and black mustache. Black stripes on the head lead to small, feathery horns that can be erected or flattened. Its black tail has white outer edges.

Natural History: If ever a bird were beautifully adapted to its habitat, it is the horned lark. Though common on prairies and farm fields, it may show up wherever patches of open, bare ground offer seeds and insects. The female builds her grassy nest in a little hollow on the bare earth, or perhaps sheltered by a dirt clod. In winter huge flocks of larks cover open ground, all walking or running (not hopping like sparrows). The Zuñi called the horned lark "snowbird" because it appeared with the snow. They also ate the lark when food was scarce during winter.

At first glance the horned lark is just another scurrying, brown bird. But watch them and you'll notice how they mill about, pecking the ground, flicking their little "horns" up to displace a neighbor. The relocated one then shoos its neighbor with a flick of the horns, and so on.

The lark family is known for its musical ability, and the male horned lark's impressive courtship display does his family proud with his musical song flight, called *larking*. Most songbirds live in wooded habitat. Here they sing from a nice perch in a tree. Horned larks are birds of treeless land. They will sing from a dirt clod or any slight rise, but to really make an impact, they perform on the wing. The male lark wings up in the air in fluttering bursts. Reaching a great height, sometimes more than 800 feet, he sings his song of tinkling notes. With his singing still audible high overhead, the male folds his wings and plummets toward the ground.

When and Where to See Them: Year-round throughout the Southwest on open ground such as deserts, shrublands, grasslands, mountain meadows, even golf courses.

Eyecatchers

The striped pattern on the head and, when visible, the lark's black feather "horns," make it look like a tiny Batman. Listen for the irregular, tinkling song, often heard even when the bird is far overhead.

Male horned lark. —WENDY SHATTIL/BOB ROZINSKI

Cactus Wren *Campylorhynchus brunneicapillus*
A.K.A.: brown-headed cactus wren   Family: Wren

Look for a large wren with rusty brown back streaked with white, dark cap with conspicuous white eyebrow, dark brown wings and tail with white bars, and paler undersides with heavily speckled breast. The tail is *not* cocked up as with most wrens.

Natural History: Spend any time at all in the desert and you'll soon wonder who is making that raucous noise. Seeming far louder than a bird this size could make, the cactus wren's call is practically the voice of the desert. Hoarse and throaty, the wren's *cha-cha-cha* or *chug-chug-chug-chug* seems to mirror the harsh landscape.

Just as you can't miss the cactus wren's voice, its nest is also a desert mainstay. True to its name, the cactus wren builds its nest in a catclaw, cholla, yucca, or other desert plants. You'll wonder how the wren managed to build its bulky, rounded nest among the nasty cactus spines. Woven of heavy fibers, the nest is covered, shaped a bit like a football, and has a side entrance. Though its setting is sharp and uncomfortable, the nest chamber is lined with soft fur and feathers. These nests may be as much as a foot in diameter. They aren't just for nesting but are used for shelter and roosting throughout the year. Cactus wrens have even been known to build their nests in clothes hanging on a clothesline. Cactus wrens may rear as many as three families a year. While the female is incubating the first clutch of eggs, the male begins building a second nest for the next brood.

Cactus wrens feed mainly on the ground, where they turn over leaves and rocks, looking for insects, and forage for seeds and berries.

When and Where to See Them: Year-round in southern Arizona, southern New Mexico, southeastern California, southern Nevada, southeastern Utah, and far western Texas, in cactus desert and arid shrublands.

Eyecatchers

The cactus wren's harsh voice, cha-cha-cha, *its striped and speckled plumage, and its white eyebrow are distinctive.*

108

Cactus wren. −MARY TAYLOR GRAY

Cactus wren nest in a cholla cactus. −MARY TAYLOR GRAY

Northern Mockingbird
A.K.A.: mimic thrush, mocker

Mimus polyglottos
Family: Mockingbird

A gray bird with paler undersides, the northern mockingbird has a long dark tail with white outer feathers, dark wings with white patches visible in flight, and a long, slender bill.

Natural History: The Latin name for the mockingbird means "many-tongued mimic," an apt name for this vocal wizard. Mocking-birds have been known to imitate the songs of 32 birds within ten minutes, as well as the calls of crickets, frogs, even the music of a piano, barking dogs, and the creaking of a rusty gate. So good are they as mimics that sonograms of their copycat sounds are indistinguishable from the real thing. In spring, male mockingbirds may sing for hours day or night, their songs highly musical with endless variations. During breeding season males confront each other at the edge of their terri-tories, hopping sideways and darting back and forth at each other. In an aerial courtship display, they fly up flashing their wing patches or fly from one perch to another, singing all the way. The mated pair forms a long-term bond.

Mockingbirds are usually associated with the South, singing from a magnolia tree amid Spanish moss. But they are a familiar sight in the Southwest, perched among the cholla and prickly pear and in shrublands up to about 5,000 feet. Both adults build the nest, of twigs, paper, wool, and other miscellany, in low shrubs and trees.

You may notice a mockingbird "flashing" the white patches on its wings by quickly opening and closing them. Biologists think this may flush out insect prey or possibly distract predators such as snakes.

When and Where to See Them: In desert and shrublands and low mountains up to about 5,000 feet, year-round throughout southern Arizona, southern New Mexico, eastern California, and far western Texas; spring through fall in northern Arizona, northern New Mexico, Utah, southwestern Colorado, and southern Nevada.

Eyecatchers

Gray and white color, long tail, and white wing patches identify the mockingbird, but its vocal repertoire is its most charming trait.

Northern mockingbird.

Curve-billed Thrasher *Toxostoma curvirostre*
A.K.A.: Palmer's thrasher   Family: Mockingbird

This is a large, ground-dwelling bird with strong legs. Note the grayish brown on back and wings, buff on the breast and belly, and long, strong, down-curved bill, orange eyes, and mottled undersides.

Natural History: The thrasher materializes from the underbrush, striding on its strong legs or running in spurts. Everything about it implies a no-nonsense approach to life, a wise attitude when you live among some of the hottest, driest terrain on the continent. There's the sturdy, sickle-shaped bill, the purposeful stride, the almost belligerent yellow eyes. In fact, the thrasher typifies desert nearly as much as the roadrunner. It is at home among cholla and prickly pear, mesquite and creosote, where it digs into the ground for insects, seeds, and berries. These thrashers often build their nests amid the bristling spines of the cholla, managing to slip through the needlelike armament without becoming impaled. You may be surprised to hear this sturdy-looking bird with the large, bold eyes that seem to stare down the world, break into a sweet series of warbles and melodies from a perch atop a cholla. But then, it is cousin to the mockingbird, a species known for its musical repertoire.

Though they live in an arid land, curve-bills are attracted to sources of water such as springs, tanks, and dripping taps. They often become quite tame around ranches as well as in picnic areas and campgrounds.

When and Where to See Them: Year-round in deserts, shrublands, and canyons in central and southern Arizona, New Mexico, far western Texas, and southeastern Utah below about 3,000 feet.

Eyecatchers

Watch for a large bird striding or running about the ground on strong legs. You can't miss the strong, curved bill and bold yellow eyes.

*Curve-billed thrasher atop a blooming
saguaro* (above) *and in a mesquite tree* (below).

Phainopepla

Phainopepla nitens

A.K.A.: black flycatcher, shining fly-snapper

Family: Silky flycatcher

These slender, glossy birds have crests, long tails, and red eyes. The male is black with white wing patches visible in flight; the female is gray.

Natural History: Phainopepla. What kind of name is that? Greek. Though intimidating to pronounce (fay-no-PEP-la), its meaning—"shining robe"—is an appropriate description of this glistening, black-robed bird.

Berries of the parasitic mistletoe plant, which lives among the branches of the mesquite tree, are a favorite food of phainopeplas. They may hover in air before a cluster of berries, or cling to the fruit clusters as they feed. Last year's nest site is often marked by a new growth of mistletoe, germinated from seeds deposited in the nest from berries fed to nestlings. Phainopeplas also fly out from a perch to snag flying insects, hence their family name, silky flycatcher.

Phainopeplas defend territories that vary in size dependent on the concentration of mistletoe berries. If berries are thick, the feeding territory is large and well defended. When resources are scattered, the birds defend only their nest tree and otherwise feed sociably with other birds. Early in spring, phainopeplas nest in lowland desert, rearing their first family of the year among the mesquite trees. In midsummer, the birds nest again amid oak woodlands and tree groves along waterways.

Phainopeplas are familiar and pleasing sights throughout much of the Southwest, particularly for winter visitors to Arizona and southwestern New Mexico. If approached, the phainopepla swoops to a perch atop a tree, perks up its crest, and sounds a throaty *quirk*.

When and Where to See Them: Year-round in southeastern California and southern Arizona; spring through fall over the rest of Arizona, southern New Mexico, the tip of Nevada, southwestern Utah, and far western Texas; in deserts and shrublands especially among mesquite trees; also in scattered woodlands along watercourses.

Eyecatchers

You'll know this jet black bird by its perky crest and red eyes. Watch for a flash of white on the wings when the male flies.

114

Male phainopepla.
—CATHY AND GORDON ILLG

Female phainopepla.
—JAN L. WASSINK

Loggerhead Shrike

Lanius ludovicianus

A.K.A.: butcher bird, cotton-picker, nine-killer

Family: Shrike

This gray-backed bird has a white breast and belly, and black wings with a white patch. A black tail with white outer feathers, a wide black stripe through the eyes, and a hooked bill distinguish this bird.

Natural History: Why is this handsome shrike nicknamed butcher bird? Though they are technically songbirds, shrikes hunt more like raptors, sitting on a low observation perch such as a fence wire or low shrub, then diving down to pounce on insects or mice, even snakes and small birds. But since they have the perching feet of a songbird, not the raptor's sharp talons, they grab their prey in their beaks, then impale them on thorns or the spikes of barbed wire, hence the nickname butcher. Though they lack strong, piercing talons, shrikes are able to carry prey with their feet. They also have excellent memories for where they have cached their meat. A report from Texas claims shrikes returned to the desiccated remains of frogs they had hung eight months earlier. Another quirk: They usually hang their prey head up.

The loggerhead shrike is often confused with the northern mockingbird. Both are black, white, and gray, with flashing white patches on their wings. Close observation will help you tell the difference. Shrikes have a larger, more rounded head, darker wings and tail, a Lone Ranger black mask across the eyes, and a shorter, heavier, slightly hooked beak.

Loggerhead shrikes are intolerant of human activity. Loggerhead populations are declining because of pesticides and loss of habitat to human development.

When and Where to See Them: Year-round throughout the Southwest in brushy open country and woodlands edging on open land.

Eyecatchers

Look closely at that robin-sized bird painted black, white, and gray, with white wing patches that flash when it flies. A hooked bill and black bandit's mask identify it as a loggerhead shrike.

116

Loggerhead shrike.

Northern Cardinal
A.K.A.: redbird

Cardinalis cardinalis
Family: Finch

The male is a bright red bird with a head crest, red beak, and black face and throat. The female is a drabber buff with red wash on her wings, crest, and tail.

Natural History: Anyone from east of the Mississippi knows the cardinal, perhaps the most familiar and identifiable songbird in North America. But did you know they are also residents of the Southwest? Don't be surprised if you're strolling in the desert and see these pointy-headed, bright red Christmas ornaments perched in a mesquite tree, as if they'd just flown out of someone's Pennsylvania backyard.

The monogamous, true-blue mating habits of cardinals seem to please humans. These little redbirds often choose the same mate year after year (not common among songbirds), returning to the same nesting territory and often remaining together the rest of the year, too. Male cardinals have gained a pugnacious reputation; not only do they attack competing males, they are also known to fly at their own reflections in windows and hubcaps. Both the male and female sing throughout the year, their song loud and whistling, with many variations (like *birdy-birdy-birdy*). During courtship they may sing soft duets, swaying slightly side by side, their crests upraised. Biologists think such avian spooning bonds the two and helps synchronize them physically for mating. But to the casual human observer, they look like any courting pair.

When and Where to See Them: Year-round through southern Arizona, southern New Mexico, and far western Texas; in open woodlands, parks, suburbs, and shrublands, often near water.

Eyecatchers

This familiar scarlet bird with the pointed crest seems to wear a flag proclaiming, "I am a cardinal!"

Female northern cardinal. ‑MARY TAYLOR GRAY

Male northern cardinal. ‑JIM CLARK

Pyrrhuloxia

A.K.A.: gray cardinal, bullfinch, parrot-bill

Cardinalis sinuatus
Family: Finch

A gray, cardinal-like bird with a peaked crest tipped in red, the male has a reddish wash down the breast, wings, and tail, and red around the eyes. The female is similar but duller, with less red.

Natural History: You just saw a gray bird that looks like a cardinal who has gone through the wash too many times (then someone went back and dipped its crest in a bucket of red paint). Well, it was almost a cardinal, a close cousin, actually. The pyrrhuloxia is the Southwest version of the cardinal. Many people have difficulty distinguishing this species from a female cardinal, but the female cardinal is buff rather than gray. The pyrrhuloxia has a down-curved beak like a parrot, colored yellow, not the pink or red of a cardinal.

Don't be put off by this species' name—pyrrhuloxia (pie-rue-LOX-ee-ah), loosely translated, means "slanting flame," a reference to the startling red-tipped crest. Alerted to danger, the male suddenly flares up his crest feathers, flashing the red tip as he calls shrilly.

It is a special treat to see pyrrhuloxias feeding on the bright red fruit of the Christmas cactus. During courtship, the male solicitously feeds bits of food to his mate, ritualized evidence of his fitness to provide for her. Later, while she incubates the eggs, he continues to feed her. The male proclaims his territory by singing a whistling, cardinal-like song. Both adults aggressively defend their territory, chasing off other birds. In fall, pyrrhuloxias band together in small flocks.

When and Where to See Them: Year-round in deserts, shrublands, and mesquite woodlands in southern Arizona, southern New Mexico, and far western Texas.

Eyecatchers

Be on the lookout for a gray cardinal, with a red-tipped crest.

Pyrrhuloxia. –JIM CLARK

Blue Grosbeak
Guiraca caerulea

A.K.A.: blue pop
Family: Finch

The male is a handsome dark blue with orange bars on the wings, the female a dull brown with blue highlights and orange wing bars. Both have the thick, heavy grosbeak bill.

Natural History: In the proper light, the male blue grosbeak is a beauty, cloaked in a deep, rich blue. But poor light robs the flashy blue bird of his showy plumage color, and he appears a dull black. That rich blue tone is, in a way, a trick of smoke and mirrors. The blue color of bird feathers is an oddity. While most colors are produced by pigments in the feathers, blue is visible to our eyes because of a filtering effect of light through the plumage. Take away the light and the bird "fades to black." Flocks of blue grosbeaks feeding on the ground are often mistaken for blackbirds or brown-headed cowbirds.

What do you notice when you see a grosbeak? Its "gross beak," of course. Meaning "big beak," this is an apt description for the heavy, sturdy bill these birds employ to crack pine nuts and other seeds. Curiously, blue grosbeaks feed to a large degree on insects and grubs, though seeds and grains are also part of their diet. They hop about, foraging on the ground and in low shrubs and trees.

During breeding season these ordinarily docile birds defend their territories from all comers. The males choose a song perch atop a tree, post, or other vantage point and sing a sweet, warbling melody that rises and falls in pitch.

When and Where to See Them: In shrubby terrain or woodland edges near open country; old, weedy fields; thickets along roads and streams; mesquite shrublands throughout the Southwest from late April through September.

Eyecatchers

A lovely dark blue bird, it has a thick bill built for heavy-duty seed cracking.

Blue grosbeak. —WENDY SHATTIL/BOB ROZINSKI

Black-throated Sparrow *Amphispiza bilineata*
A.K.A.: desert sparrow, black-throat   **Family: Finch**

White underparts and white lines above the eyes identify this otherwise gray-brown sparrow. White lines along the sides of the neck outline a distinctive black triangle on the throat.

Natural History: "Some like it hot" might be the motto of the black-throated sparrow, for these birds inhabit the driest, hottest deserts of the land, even Death Valley. They forage among the creosote, agave, and saguaro, eating insects, seeds, plant shoots, and green growth. So well are they adapted to an arid habitat, these sparrows can survive in some seasons without drinking water, gaining the moisture they need from their food. Ecologically, this allows them to live in a land where few others can survive, thereby reducing competition for resources.

The deserts and shrublands of the Southwest are alive with black-throated sparrows, but to see them up close, be sure to have your binoculars along. These birds are shy, fast, and won't tolerate your coming too near. From a distance, the black-throat looks like any other little brown bird, but focused in the binoculars it's quite striking. A large throat patch resembles the black spade from a playing card. White lines radiate from the beak, streaking over each eye and outlining each side of the black throat. Unlike many other songbird species where the male is flashy and the female drab, the male and female black-throated sparrow look the same.

Keep your binocs trained and you'll be surprised to see a black-throat leap suddenly to grab at a seedhead bobbing above its head, snatching a seed before falling back to the ground.

When and Where to See Them: Throughout deserts and dry, open country of the Southwest, particularly on rocky slopes; year-round in low-lying areas, spring through fall in northern and higher-elevation regions.

Eyecatchers

The black throat patch is shaped like the black spade on a playing card.

124

Black-throated sparrow. –TOM J. ULRICH

White-crowned Sparrow *Zonotrichia leucophrys*
A.K.A.: white-crown, Gambel's sparrow   Family: Finch

The white-crown is a grayish brown sparrow with rusty wings and a black head with bright, white stripes.

Natural History: Winter is the time to see white-crowns in the Southwest, as they gather in flocks of up to 50 birds in parks, streamside thickets, and residential landscaping, filling the shrubs with activity and their pert *jip* calls. Wearing a black helmet prominently striped with white, the head feathers often lifted in a slight crest, the white-crown is not easily confused with any other sparrow. Researchers have found these head stripes are important to an individual's status within the white-crown community. Birds with the brightest black-and-white stripes hold positions of greatest dominance whereas those with dull stripes, typical of juvenile birds, are low on the totem pole. When researchers used paint to brighten the head stripes of the low dogs, their social status went up.

Like many human "snowbirds" arriving in the Southwest with the winter, white-crowned sparrows migrate from northern nesting grounds in the western United States, Canada, and Alaska (and, yes, they show up on resort golf courses of the sunshine belt). Wintering white-crowns often form large, mixed flocks with black-throated, Brewer's, and sage sparrows. Scientists think this helps the birds better protect themselves from predators and feed more efficiently.

When and Where to See Them: From late September through April throughout the Southwest in open woodlands, shrublands, city parks, and backyard shrubbery, often near water.

Eyecatchers

The black head is boldly striped from front to back with white.

White-crowned sparrow.

Western Meadowlark

Sturnella neglecta
Family: Troupial

This grayish brown bird has a bright yellow breast and a black V across the chest.

Natural History: As winter fades from the grasslands and open country of the Southwest, a gray-and-yellow bird feels the springtime urge to mate. Though it has lived among the weeds, grasses, and shrubs all winter, it has kept silent, foraging for food and surviving the cold months. Now the land is reawakening, and the meadowlark offers the world a gift—its wonderful song. Bobbing on top of a weed stalk or perched on a post or fence wire along a country road, the male meadowlark tosses back his head and sings. His song is rich, fluting, and joyful, spilling across the grassland, as bright as the western sunshine.

The male performs his courtship display on the ground in front of the female. He fluffs up his breast and fans his tail and wings, jerking the tail up and down and waving first one wing, then the other, or perhaps both together. With his bill pointed skyward to display his bright yellow breast and the black chevron on his chest, he jumps straight up.

As residents of treeless terrain, meadowlarks build their nests on the ground from dried plant fibers, well hidden among the grass. The nest is domed, has a side entrance, and is often approached by tunnels through the grass. When the female is sitting on the eggs she may not flush until practically stepped on.

The **eastern meadowlark** is also common in the Southwest. It is very similar in appearance to the western but can be distinguished by its song—a clear, high-pitched whistle.

When and Where to See Them: Year-round throughout the Southwest in open grasslands, farmlands, and shrublands, and along roadsides.

Eyecatchers

The fluting call of the western meadowlark—chir chirtly chirtly chir—is surely the song of western open spaces. Watch for its bright yellow breast marked by a black V, and the white flash of the outer tail feathers when the bird flies.

128

Western meadowlark.

Great-tailed Grackle

Quiscalus mexicanus

A.K.A.: jackdaw, crow blackbird

Family: Troupial

The male is a large black bird with iridescent greenish purple plumage, yellow eyes, a long, strong bill, and a long tail. The female is brown, with pale underparts and eyestripe, dark eyes, and an average-size tail.

Natural History: Grackles are almost as renowned for their voices as their bold appearance. Wander under a grackle roost tree and you'll think you've arrived in a busy native market in some exotic locale. Squawking, squealing, cracking, shrieking, singing, shouting—the grackle's repertoire of sounds is truly amazing (and annoying, if you have to listen to it too long). The male's appearance matches his voice as he promenades with his long tail sweeping behind him like a regal robe. Even the way he surveys the world with his startling yellow eyes seems bold. By contrast the female is smaller than the male and an unremarkable brown with little metallic sheen to her plumage. Yet attracting her attention becomes the male's preoccupation during the breeding season. He fluffs his feathers, fans his long tail, and vibrates his wings, serenading her with his raucous voice. Males mate with numerous females and leave the mothers with all the duties of child-rearing. Females build their nests near each other in colonies of up to thousands of grackles. They often squabble with each other over nest sites and steal nesting materials from their neighbors.

Grackles are another species that has expanded its range with human development, spreading north from Mexico along river valleys deforested for agriculture, and across irrigated farmland.

When and Where to See Them: Year-round in southern Arizona, southern New Mexico, southeastern California, far western Texas, and the southern tip of Nevada, ranging into northern Arizona, northern New Mexico, and southern Colorado spring through fall. Grackles inhabit grasslands and farmlands with scattered stands of trees near water, and marshes with tall trees.

Eyecatchers

You'll know this bird by its large size and the male's glossy, iridescent plumage, long tail, and amazing vocal abilities.

130

Great-tailed grackle. –MARY TAYLOR GRAY

Hooded Oriole

A.K.A.: palm oriole

Icterus cucullatus

Family: Troupial

The male is a very brightly colored, orange-yellow oriole with black upper back and wings and a distinctively marked black mask and throat spreading down the upper breast. The female is greenish yellow with darker wings.

Natural History: Each spring groups of orioles show up in the Southwest, and they're not the baseball-playing kind dropping by for spring training. The hooded oriole is a handsome, brightly colored, southwestern version of the much more widespread **northern oriole.** Because it prefers to nest in the fanlike leaves of native desert palms, especially in watered canyons of the southeastern California deserts, the hooded oriole is sometimes called the palm oriole. By planting palm trees for landscaping, humans have helped the hooded oriole expand its range. In true Californian style, where the palm tree oases of real estate developers pop up in the desert, so do the hooded orioles. They build typical oriole nests—pendulous pouches of grass and plant fibers suspended from a branch or, if in a palm, from an overhanging frond.

Orioles are fruit and nectar eaters. Equipped with long, powerful bills, they poke through the bases of the blossoms of agaves, lilies, hibiscus, and other tubular flowers instead of "dipping and sipping" like the needle-billed hummingbird. Orioles will come to halves of oranges and grapefruits left out for them, as well as make use of the nectar in hummingbird feeders. They also eat many insects. The **Scott's oriole,** a close cousin of the hooded, is a similar southwestern oriole with black head and back, black-and-white wings, and yellow underparts.

When and Where to See Them: In sycamore, cottonwood, and oak woodlands along waterways, in towns, and on ranches and in palm groves from late March through September in central and southern Arizona, southern New Mexico, southeastern California, southern Nevada, and far western Texas.

Eyecatchers

You can't miss the male's bright orange-yellow coloring, contrasted with its black wings and bold, black throat.

Male hooded oriole. Orioles will feed on fresh fruit set out for them and sometimes drink from hummingbird feeders. –MARY TAYLOR GRAY

Female hooded oriole. –MARY TAYLOR GRAY

House Finch
A.K.A.: rose-breasted finch,
Mexican house finch, red-head

Carpodacus mexicanus
Family: Finch

The male is gray brown with a bright red or orange cap, throat, and rump. The gray-brown female has a streaked underside.

Natural History: You probably are familiar with house finches, but did you know they are common birds of the Southwest? Whereas many bird species have retreated before the advance of human development, the house finch has thrived. Well named, the house finch takes full advantage of urban and suburban landscaping and the food and water that come with it. In fact, a large part of the house finch's diet is seeds from weeds like thistle and dandelion introduced by humans. But finches don't just lounge around feeders for easy handouts. Stroll out in the deserts and canyons and you'll find these pretty birds with the lovely, fluting song surviving amid the cholla, saguaro, and mesquite.

A range map for the house finch shows an interesting polarity—a broad distribution in the Southwest and West, and a second distribution along the East Coast. How did this happen? Bright as a Christmas tree ornament, the red-dipped male house finch caught the eye of caged-bird traders. In the 1940s, a cargo of house finches was brought illegally into New York City, and ended up on the loose on Long Island. These birds of the southwestern deserts established a breeding population and before long had spread throughout the eastern United States.

Watch the house finches at your feeder and notice how the males range in color from bright scarlet to orange to dark yellow. In spring and summer their cheery, whistling song is a delight. Leave out bits of cotton or soft fur combed from your pets for the female to use in nest building; you may be rewarded with a house finch nest near your home.

When and Where to See Them: Year-round in deserts, shrublands, lower reaches of canyons, and cities, towns, and suburbs throughout the Southwest.

Eyecatchers

The bright red throat, head, and rump of the male stand out on what is otherwise a nondescript little brown bird.

House finches, like the male shown here, are common feeder birds. –JIM CLARK

House finches live year-round throughout the Southwest. –JIM CLARK

BIRDS OF THE
HIGH COUNTRY

▼▼▼▼▼▼▼▼▼▼▼▼

Mountains, Mesas,
and Canyons

Golden eagle
Peregrine falcon
Wild turkey
White-throated swift
Acorn woodpecker
Cliff swallow
Steller's jay
Gray-breasted jay
Common raven
Bridled titmouse
White-breasted nuthatch
Canyon wren
Western bluebird
Yellow-rumped warbler
Painted redstart
Dark-eyed junco

Golden Eagle

Aquila chrysaetos

A.K.A.: mountain eagle,
ring-tailed eagle, royal eagle

Family: Hawk

The adult is a large brown eagle with golden brown wash on the back of the head and neck. Immature birds have a white band at the base of the tail. The beak and head are smaller than the bald eagle, but the tail is longer. The legs of the golden eagle, a dry-land hunter, are feathered down to the feet, while the bald eagle, primarily a fisher, has bare, unfeathered legs.

Natural History: In Native American legend, the golden eagle passes through a hole in the sky to visit with the gods, returning with messages for lesser, earth-bound creatures. With its powerful form, regal bearing, and effortless grace in the sky, it's easy to believe this magnificent hunter is indeed a magic being.

The golden eagle is a living metaphor of the wild country it inhabits, a land of high and lonesome mountains, plunging cliffs and rocky canyons. From a rock ledge or mesa top, the golden eagle surveys its territory, launching out with a flapping of great wings that can span seven and a half feet. Golden eagles can soar for hours on rising currents of warm air, carving graceful circles beneath the clouds, then spiraling higher until no more than a speck in the sky. Spotting prey on the ground, the golden eagle stoops like a falcon, plummeting at speeds estimated at up to 200 mph, and grabbing its prey in powerful talons. Stockmen have long feared golden eagle predation on lambs, calves, and kids, and thousands of golden eagles were killed annually to protect livestock before the Bald Eagle Act was amended in 1962 to provide federal protection for golden eagles. However, a 1966 study in Montana sheep country found no evidence of predation by golden eagles. In fact, rabbits comprised 70 percent of the birds' diet. Despite their aristocratic demeanor, golden eagles do not have a discriminating palate and will eat everything from insects to carrion.

Mated for life, the golden eagle pair defends a hunting territory averaging 36 square miles, where they nest each year. Though associated with mountains and canyons, golden eagles often hunt over open country and are seen perched atop poles along country roads. Don't

continued

*Golden eagle. Note the golden plumage
on the nape of its neck.* –TERRY WYGANT

Golden Eagle
continued

Aquila chrysaetos

expect to hear a piercing scream from a golden eagle. Like the bald eagle, the golden's voice, when heard, is a weak mewing with occasional yelps and squeals.

When and Where to See Them: Year-round in mountain, canyon, and mesa country, and nearby open land throughout the Southwest.

Eyecatchers

Its very large size and dark brown plumage distinguish this spectacular bird. The golden eagle soars on large, broad wings held in a straight line (the turkey vulture holds its wings tipped up). Mountain and dryland habitat help distinguish it from an immature bald eagle.

Golden eagle. –TERRY WYGANT

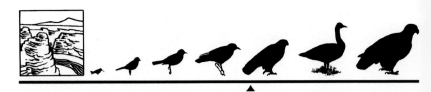

Peregrine Falcon
A.K.A.: duck hawk, wandering falcon

Falco peregrinus
Family: Falcon

This large falcon has slate blue back and wings; pale underparts with blue-gray barring; black head and back of neck; dark, curved bar or "whisker" on pale cheek; long dark tail; long tapering wings.

Natural History: The recovery of this magnificent falcon is one of the success stories of wildlife conservation. By the early 1970s the peregrine had disappeared from most of its former range throughout the lower 48 states, the victim of DDT and other pesticides that accumulated through the food chain and poisoned the falcon by making the shells of its eggs too thin to survive incubation. An intense recovery effort, launched practically in the eleventh hour, included the introduction of captive-bred young into wild nests. Imagine the commitment of the biologists who scaled cliffs to reach the wild aeries, risking the wrath of the adults, to install those fragile chicks in cliff-top nests. By 1994 the peregrine falcon had rebounded sufficiently for the Arctic peregrine falcon subspecies to be removed from the endangered species list.

To witness a peregrine falcon perched on a cliff edge, knowing you are viewing a rare species once close to extinction, is a thrill. Should you see the swift, blue-gray falcons hunting you'll be convinced of the intangible value of wild places and wild things. Falcons eat mainly other birds, plummeting upon them from above at high speed. The falcon's dive, or "stoop," can exceed 150 mph. The hunter strikes its prey with open talons, ripping loose a shower of feathers. The quarry is then retrieved from the ground or sometimes is grabbed in midair.

When and Where to See Them: Year-round in canyons and cliffs, often near water; in mountains of Arizona, New Mexico, southern Utah, southwestern Colorado; Grand Canyon National Park and Canyon de Chelly National Monument in Arizona and Mesa Verde National Park in Colorado.

Eyecatchers

Look for its large size, slate blue plumage, and characteristic cheek stripe, or whisker. In flight watch for the falcon's tapered wings, rapid wing beats, and dramatic stoop on aerial prey.

Peregrine falcon. −WENDY SHATTIL/BOB ROZINSKI

Wild Turkey
A.K.A.: tom turkey, gobbler, wood turkey

Meleagris gallopavo
Family: Turkey

A very large, iridescent bronze bird with a naked blue head and red "wattles" (loose throat skin), fleshy snood dangling from above the bill, and a feathery "beard" hanging from the breast, the male is as much as four feet tall, the female three feet.

Natural History: Certainly the wild turkey must be the most American of birds. It fed the Pilgrims at the first Thanksgiving and was nominated by Ben Franklin to be our nation's symbol because, though "vain and silly," it was courageous (by contrast, he considered the bald eagle a bird of bad moral character). But the wild turkey has an older history with even earlier Americans. The turkeys of the Southwest were domesticated by the Anasazi, who inhabited the cliff dwellings and pueblos of Canyon de Chelly, Chaco Canyon, Mesa Verde, and innumerable other sites throughout much of the Southwest until about A.D.1400. Turkeys are birds of the New World, unknown in Europe until taken there from Mexico in the early 1500s by Spanish conquistadors. Domestic turkeys spread across Europe, returning to the New World with European settlers as barnyard fowl.

Turkeys were once abundant and widely distributed in the United States, estimated to number ten million before the arrival of Columbus. Relentless hunting combined with destruction of their woodland habitat led to their extirpation in more than a dozen eastern states. Always a popular game bird, turkeys have been reintroduced over much of their former range as well as in new areas.

A tom turkey in full display is a spectacle to behold. He puffs out his body feathers and fans his tail like a peacock, dropping his wings and rattling his feathers. His head and neck wattles flush red, and he gobbles and struts back and forth on parade in an effort to attract females for mating. Turkeys may gobble in any season, but spring is true gobbling time, when the fine gobble of a prime tom can be heard a mile away.

Wild turkeys are wary birds. They fly well for short distances, but are mainly ground dwellers, foraging in the dirt and leaf litter for insects, acorns, and other food. Your best chance to see them is probably morning and evening when they roost in flocks in trees, although in

continued

Male wild turkey displaying. Note the red and blue head and neck, fleshy "snood" dangling from above the bill, and plumed "beard" projecting from the chest. −WENDY SHATTIL/BOB ROZINSKI

Wild Turkey
continued

Meleagris gallopavo

areas where they are used to humans they seem to materialize out of the woods, walking along seemingly unmindful of humans.

According to Native American legend, the turkey and the turkey vulture, both naked-headed birds, lost their head feathers helping to push the sun into the sky.

When and Where to See Them: Year-round in open pine and oak woodlands of the canyons and mountains of central and northern Arizona and New Mexico, southwestern Colorado, southern Utah, and far western Texas.

Eyecatchers

Watch for the main course of Thanksgiving dinner strutting about in the wild.

Female wild turkey. –STEVE RENZI

White-throated Swift   *Aeronautes saxatalis*

Family: Swift

This swift is a black, swallowlike bird with white throat, breast, and belly, and white patches under the wings and down the sides. It has long, slender, pointed wings, slightly forked tail, and short bill.

Natural History: Watch the air above any rocky canyon and you're liable to see white-throated swifts swooping and arcing, flashing here, then abruptly changing direction. The wings of swifts are adapted for high-speed flight—long, narrow, pointed, and curving backward; they are likely the fastest-flying bird in North America. One observation of a swift eluding the diving stoop of a peregrine falcon estimated the swift's escape speed at 200 mph. Swifts are creatures of the air, seeming to live their lives on the wing. They feed in flight. Their wide, gaping mouths, which open clear back under their eyes, help them snap flying insects from the air. Swifts court and even mate on the wing. Their legs and feet are so weak they may have trouble taking off again if they should land on the ground. In fact this family's Latin name, Apodidae, means "without feet." Though they resemble swallows, which are songbirds, swifts are actually more closely related to hummingbirds. It's easy to mistake a white-throated swift for a **violet-green swallow,** which may share its habitat. Watch for black-and-white markings on the swift's belly; the swallow is all white below.

Listen for the high-pitched cries of swifts as they echo off the canyon walls—a chuckling *he, he, he, he.* White-throated swifts are consummate canyon creatures, nesting on inaccessible ledges and cliff faces, their feather and grass cup nests glued to the rock with the adults' saliva.

When and Where to See Them: In canyons, cliffs, and mountainous terrain throughout the Southwest. Year-round in much of the Southwest but only during summer in colder, northern mountains.

Eyecatchers

Dramatically clothed in black and white, the swift cuts and wheels above a canyon on long, slender wings like a flying scimitar.

148

The white-throated swift is almost always seen in flight high above a canyon or rocky cliff. –H. CLARKE/VIREO

Acorn Woodpecker

A.K.A.: ant-eating woodpecker

Melanerpes formicivorus

Family: Woodpecker

This black woodpecker has a bright red cap and boldly marked black head contrasted by white forehead, cheeks, and throat, white wing patches and rump, and yellow eyes.

Natural History: Acorn woodpeckers are well named. They live in colonies of 2 to 15 birds (often extended families of pairs and their offspring), and acorns figure prominently in their lives. In the fall, these harlequin hammerers work together to prepare for winter. They drill holes in trees, then wedge acorns and other nuts in the crevices. Conserving time and labor, the birds reuse storage holes in successive years. The stashed acorns provide food for the woodpecker group to survive winter, and they guard it well. If squirrels, titmice, or Lewis' woodpeckers, which also store acorns, raid their stored booty, the acorn woodpeckers attack. Within acorn woodpecker territory, sit and watch the birds for a while and you'll observe them returning repeatedly to the same trees with acorns or other booty to store. You will probably hear their tapping as they drill holes or tap nuts into place (a sound represented by the Zuñi word for woodpecker—*tamtununu*). Listen also for their loud, characteristic call, described as *JA-cob* or *WAKE-up*.

The extended family cooperates in child-rearing, taking turns incubating eggs and feeding the nestlings. As with many species dependent on particular seed crops, acorn woodpecker populations cycle with the acorns. In an abundant year, the flock rears many young, but if a crop fails, the numbers of acorn woodpeckers also decline.

Like other woodpeckers, these also eat insects. In fact, part of this species' Latin name, *formicivorus*, means "ant eater."

When and Where to See Them: In oak and oak-pine woodlands; year-round in most of Arizona and New Mexico except for northern mountains, and in far western Texas.

Eyecatchers

This woodpecker's "clown face" is boldly patterned in black, white, and red, with startling yellow eyes. Watch for the flash of white on the wings when it flies.

Acorn woodpecker.   –PAUL A. BERQUIST

Cliff Swallow

Hirundo pyrrhonota

A.K.A.: crescent swallow, mud swallow

Family: Swallow

This blue-black swallow has a white forehead, rust red face and rump, white belly, grayish sides, and square tail.

Natural History: Cliff swallows are part of a romantic story. They're the faithful swallows that return each March to the Mission of San Juan Capistrano in southern California in what is now a busy suburb of Los Angeles. The actual arrival date varies sometimes from the March 19 of legend, depending on weather and other factors. Since 1776 the birds have returned each spring to nest under the eaves of the old mission.

Unlike birds such as the whooping crane that can't tolerate human activity, the cliff swallow has benefited from human settlement. Forests cut for farmland mean more insects and hunting terrain for these aerial predators. Barns, homes, and bridges provide nesting habitat, and colonies of more than 1,000 nests housing thousands of birds have been recorded. In turn, swallows benefit humans, eating great numbers of insects, including agricultural pests like boll weevils.

Cliff swallow colonies are like avian cliff dwellings, the nests glued like mud gourds beneath overhangs, their gooseneck entrances peering every which way. The airspace below the colony is an explosion of aerial sound and activity. Swallows take off, swoop fore and aft, bank and wheel in the air, flashing pale bellies as they pitch and glide. The adults zoom in to pop headfirst into their mud houses, carrying food to their young. After a moment their round, wide-lipped heads appear in the entrance before they launch once more into space.

Other common swallows in the Southwest include the swallow-tailed **barn swallow**, the blue-backed, white-breasted **tree swallow**, the **rough-winged swallow**, and the **violet-green swallow**.

When and Where to See Them: From early April through September throughout the Southwest; around cliffs, bridges, dams, and rural structures, often near water.

Eyecatchers

The white forehead, square tail, and rusty red coloration are distinctive of this blue-black swallow.

Adult cliff swallows gather dabs of mud with their bills and construct their nests bit by bit, like a mason building a brick wall.
—JAN L. WASSINK

Cliff swallows nest in busy, clustered colonies of mud nests glued beneath cliffs, bridges, and overhangs.
—JAN L. WASSINK

Steller's Jay

A.K.A.: mountain blue jay

Cyanocitta stelleri

Family: Crow

You may hear this handsome, very blue mountain jay with a black head and crest before you see it.

Natural History: If you're in ponderosa pine forest in the high country of the Southwest, you'll soon encounter a bold and handsome bird dressed in blue, its head crowned with a fine black crest—the Steller's jay. You never need be in doubt of the identification of this bird. It is the only crested jay in the mountain West. Many visitors unfamiliar with this western mountain jay mistakenly call it a blue jay, a close cousin whose range, until recently, did not extend west of the Mississippi. Another all-blue jay, the **pinyon jay,** lacks a crest and is found most often in pinyon-juniper forest rather than ponderosa pine.

The Steller's jay often materializes suddenly in the pine forest, especially around a picnic site. Watch how the trees soon fill with jays, who fly from ground to stump to tree limb looking for a vantage point. Steller's jays eat mainly pine nuts, seeds, and fruits as well as insects, grubs, and the eggs and nestlings of other birds. They sometimes pirate the stored acorns of acorn woodpeckers.

The Steller's jay's harsh voice, a familiar sound in mountain forests, is typical of the crow family. To many ears it sounds demanding and quarrelsome. Steller's jays also produce a scream much like that of a red-tailed hawk or golden eagle, perhaps to frighten smaller birds from their nests, leaving the eggs and young open to attack. By contrast, when around their own nests they are quiet and retiring.

When and Where to See Them: In canyon and mountain coniferous forests of Arizona, New Mexico, southern Utah, Colorado, southern Nevada, and far western Texas, spring through fall, moving to lower-elevation oak-pine forests in winter. In years when the pine seed crop is poor, they may "irrupt" into the Arizona deserts.

Eyecatchers

The electric blue color and black crest of this jay are unmistakable. Its harsh voice—shaak, shaak, shaak!—so at odds with its elegant appearance, often announces its presence.

Steller's jay. —JIM CLARK

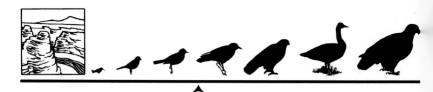

Gray-breasted Jay

A.K.A.: Mexican jay, Arizona jay

Aphelocoma ultramarina

Family: Crow

The gray-breasted jay is gray blue with light gray undersides, long tail, and a smooth, crest-less head.

Natural History: You're looking at a large, handsome bluish jay with a pale underside and no crest. You consult your field guide and find two western jays that look like the one begging food at your picnic table. Location will help you decide if the jay you're looking at is the gray-breasted jay or its more common and widespread cousin the **scrub jay.** If you're not in the mountains of central or southern Arizona, southwestern New Mexico, or southwestern Texas, you're looking at a scrub jay. The scrub jay also has a whitish throat and eyebrow and is a little more slender. It helps to hear their voices—the scrub jay's is more raspy, the gray-breasted's higher pitched and inquisitive.

Like most jays, gray-breasteds are bold and gregarious, with loud, harsh voices. You'll often find them around campgrounds and picnic sites, where they have learned to beg for handouts and clean up the leftovers. These are mountain birds, living in oak and pine forests between about 2,000 and 9,000 feet. They are particularly common in the mountain ranges around Tucson and points south.

Gray-breasted jays live in flocks of close relatives, several pairs often nesting near each other. Young from previous broods often help their parents feed the next batch of nestlings. Predators that draw too near the nests, even ones who innocently stop for a nap near the wrong tree, are mobbed and attacked by screaming flocks of jays.

When and Where to See Them: Year-round in oak and pine forests in the hills and mountains of southern Arizona, the southwestern corner of New Mexico, and far western Texas, including Big Bend National Park.

Eyecatchers

Look for a large, blue-backed, gregarious jay without a crest.

Gray-breasted jays, like other members of the jay family, are common picnic visitors. –MARY TAYLOR GRAY

Common Raven
A.K.A.: American raven

Corvus corax
Family: Crow

The raven is a very large, black crowlike bird with a strong, arched bill and shaggy throat feathers.

Natural History: Perhaps it is the raven's coal black, preacher's-suit plumage. Maybe it is the bird's all-knowing demeanor, its boldness, or the way it sits just out of reach but unafraid. Whatever the allure, the raven figures in the folklore of cultures worldwide, as sage, deity, omen. To some Native Americans, Raven was the creator and their ancestor. In the Bible, Noah loosed a raven to test the flood waters. To poet Edgar Allan Poe a raven was the midnight visitor that quoth "Nevermore!"

Ravens are found throughout the Southwest in a variety of habitats: canyons, mountain forests, deserts, open country. Their nests are big, loose jumbles of sticks, wool, bones, and other material, typically built on a cliff but also in trees or even the saguaro cactus. Ravens are the largest songbirds (passerines, or perching birds) in the world.

Spring is a great time to watch ravens, especially in canyon country. Here the males soar, circle, and tumble for the female. At times the air space above a narrow canyon seems filled with black ravens, their shadows slicing across the canyon walls and their raucous, hollow calls echoing among the rocks. The raven pair mates for life and may soar together, wingtips touching. Though biologists are reluctant to admit animals might play, they think some of the raven's soaring and diving is indeed play behavior. Ravens often circle hawklike on rising air thermals. Their smaller, straight-billed heads distinguish them from hawks and their flat wings from tilt-winged vultures.

A close cousin of the widespread common raven, the smaller **Chihuahuan raven** (formerly called the white-necked raven) lives among the shrublands of the Southwest, along the Mexican border. Even expert birders would have difficulty distinguishing it from the common raven, in fact the Zuñi refer to the ravens as "two birds, one name." The white underfeathers on the neck of the Chihuahuan are sometimes visible. This raven gathers in enormous flocks of up to 100 birds whereas the common raven is usually seen singly, in pairs, or small groups.

continued

Common raven. –TOM J. ULRICH

Common Raven

continued

Corvus corax

When and Where to See Them: Year-round throughout the Southwest in canyons, mountains, coniferous forests, deserts, shrublands, and open country.

Eyecatchers

This large, handsome, glossy black bird can be distinguished from a crow by its larger size. In flight, look for the end of the tail shaped in a wedge, rather than straight across like a crow's.

Chihuahuan raven (photo taken at the Arizona-Sonora Desert Museum). –MARY TAYLOR GRAY

Bridled Titmouse
A.K.A.: Wollweber's titmouse

Parus wollweberi
Family: Titmouse

A small, light gray songbird with darker wings, the bridled titmouse has a dark head crest, black bib, and pattern of black lines on the head.

Natural History: If this sprightly, crested little mountain bird hopping busily among scrub oak, juniper, pine, and sycamore groves reminds you of the **black-capped chickadee,** it's no surprise because they're cousins, members of the titmouse family. Bridled titmice remind us of chickadees not just in their small size and bright manner, but in their gray-and-black coloration, black markings, and even their call—a harsh, high-pitched *chick-a-dee.* They also whistle a high, two-note *fee-bee,* another chickadee-like trait.

The bridled titmouse thrives in the hill country of Mexico clear down into the highlands of Guatemala. In the United States, you'll find bridled titmice only in the hills and mountains of southern Arizona and southwestern New Mexico. They favor forests and open woodlands between about 5,000 and 7,000 feet, where they forage in small flocks and family groups. Though a bit more shy than others of its family (you may well hear it before you see it), the bridled titmouse is a staunch defender of home and hearth. The threat of an owl, hawk, or other predator in the neighborhood brings out a chattering, mobbing flock of bridled titmice, ready to do battle.

When and Where to See Them: Spring through fall in mountain and foothill forests and open woodlands, especially among pine and oak, descending into wooded valleys in winter; in southern Arizona and southwestern New Mexico.

Eyecatchers

The pattern of lines on the face suggest a horse's bridle, and the bird sports a pert blackish head crest.

162

Bridled titmouse. −D. AND M. ZIMMERMAN/VIREO

The familiar and widespread black-capped chickadee is a close relative of the titmouse. −JAN L. WASSINK

White-breasted Nuthatch *Sitta carolinensis*

A.K.A.: topsy-turvy bird,   Family: Nuthatch
tree mouse, devil-down-head

This blue-gray bird has white undersides and head and black cap spreading down the back of the neck. The head flows into the body with little definable neck; its slender bill often points in line with the body.

Natural History: Nuthatches never fail to delight observers as they travel headfirst down the trunks of trees. This unique habit has been celebrated in their many whimsical nicknames—topsy-turvy bird, devil-down-head. With a foraging style all their own (nuthatches are the only birds that forage by traveling down tree trunks), they search nooks and crannies for insects overlooked by birds that travel up, such as woodpeckers and creepers.

Nuthatches usually attract your notice as a flitting bit of activity moving nervously about the limbs or trunk of a tree. The nuthatch pair raises their family, then stays together on the same small territory through the winter, foraging separately but keeping in touch by calling to each other. Listen for their call in mountain and canyon forests, a rapid, high-pitched *yank, yank, yank*. After the breeding season, nuthatches sometimes form mixed feeding flocks with chickadees, creepers, and woodpeckers; biologists think this may provide safety in numbers as well as allow the large group of birds to feed in territories that they would be chased out of (by the resident bird) on their own.

A smaller cousin, the **pygmy nuthatch,** inhabits mountain pine forests. It has a brown cap that comes below the eyes. The **red-breasted nuthatch** has a rusty breast and black line through the eye.

When and Where to See Them: In mountain and canyon forests of conifers, oak, and sycamore year-round throughout the Southwest.

Eyecatchers

Watch for a nervous, busy creature flitting about the branches or trunk of a tree, traveling head down. *The white breast, face, and neck, and bold black cap and nape distinguish this from other nuthatches.*

White-breasted nuthatch traveling headfirst down a tree trunk.
—WENDY SHATTIL/BOB ROZINSKI

Nuthatch peering from a nest cavity.
—JIM CLARK

Canyon Wren

A.K.A.: dotted wren, bugler

Catherpes mexicanus
Family: Wren

Canyon wrens are brownish red with a white throat and breast, chestnut belly, speckled plumage, and an upcocked tail with black rings.

Natural History: The song of the canyon wren is without doubt among the prettiest music of the natural world. Cascading melodiously down the scale like water bubbling down a rocky streambed, the canyon wren's song is a perfect musical interpretation of its canyon habitat. Hiking in canyon country, the wren's voice invariably stops nature lovers in their tracks, evoking a delighted, "Listen, there's a canyon wren."

Actually, you are much more likely to hear this wren than see it, though cautious stalking, following the repeated call, can often bring you to the source. The Acoma Indians characterized the canyon wren, with its loud voice that booms off canyon walls, as a town crier.

Canyon wrens are typically wrenlike in appearance—large head that flows into thick shoulders with little evidence of a neck, long pointed bill, small eye, and pert, upcocked tail with black bands. Canyon wrens inhabit rough, rocky, watered canyons, probing in rock crevices with their long bills for insects and other invertebrates. Very little is actually known about this attractive bird's natural history—nesting, diet, displays, and other elements of its life history are in need of much further study.

When and Where to See Them: Year-round throughout the Southwest in steep, rocky canyons usually marked by flowing water.

Eyecatchers

Listen for the melodious, whistling song of this canyon dweller, which cascades down the scale in liquid notes—pooeep, pueep, pueep, pueep.

166

Canyon wren. –JIM CLARK

Western Bluebird

A.K.A.: Mexican bluebird

Sialia mexicana
Family: Thrush

The male is a handsome bird colored deep blue with a reddish breast and upper back, and pale, whitish belly. The female is brownish gray with some red on her breast and sides.

Natural History: With their strong coloring, these birds, whether western, eastern, or mountain, deserve to bear the title of "blue bird." West of the Mississippi, the western bluebird replaces the eastern, although a subspecies of eastern bluebird is resident in the mountains at the southern edge of Arizona.

Bluebirds are insect eaters, fluttering from a perch at the edge of open ground to grab flying insects. Like their cousin the robin, they also eat worms, snails, fruits, and berries.

Loss of nesting sites has greatly harmed bluebird populations throughout the United States. Bluebirds depend on holes in trees and posts for sheltered nest spots. Loss of dead standing trees and the removal of dead branches by humans, as well as the replacement of wooden fence posts with iron posts, have reduced the amount of nesting habitat. Competition with other cavity-nesting birds, especially aggressive, introduced species such as house sparrows and starlings, has also hurt the gentle bluebird's nesting success. Programs to provide nest boxes along "bluebird trails" in rural and suburban communities on both public and private land are helping all three bluebird species. Such programs demonstrate the value and importance of individual, landowner, and community involvement in wildlife conservation.

Eastern bluebirds are very similar to western, but the red breast color extends up the throat. **Mountain bluebirds** are sky blue with gray-blue breasts.

When and Where to See Them: Open woodlands near grasslands and farmland, shrublands, and brushy deserts. Year-round throughout the Southwest except in deserts of southern Arizona and far western Texas, where they are winter residents in stands of mistletoe-mesquite.

Eyecatchers

You can't miss the deep blue coloring of the male, punctuated by chestnut chest and upper back.

168

Western bluebird.

Yellow-rumped Warbler *Dendroica coronata*
A.K.A.: Audubon's warbler   Family: Warbler

The male is charcoal gray with a yellow cap, throat, and rump; yellow patches on the sides; whitish undersides; and white tail patches. The female is similar but duller, without as much eyecatching yellow.

Natural History: One of the fun things about yellow-rumped warblers is how easy they are to see. Warblers are small birds; many are not conspicuously colored, and their habits may keep them hidden from our eyes. Southwestern warblers, such as **Grace's warbler** and **Lucy's warbler,** aren't uncommon but one inhabits the tops of trees, and the other is active by dawn and dusk, so you will rarely notice them. But venture out in a pine or fir forest in summer and you'll likely run into many boldly colored yellow-rumps moving busily about the trees.

Yellow-rumped warblers are known for the way they zip from a tree, arcing up after a cloud of flying insects. In summer when resources are abundant in their mountain forests, the warblers swarm in flocks over the coniferous trees, ferreting out the insects hiding in, on, and around the vegetation. In winter, the flocks thin out to a few birds. As they forage, the yellow-rump flock keeps in constant contact with a terse *chip.*

The eastern and western races of this species formerly were considered distinctly separate species. The Myrtle warbler was familiar in the East, the Audubon's warbler in the West. But as the prairies of the central United States were developed, trees began to link the two wooded halves of the country. The Myrtle and Audubon's warblers were found to interbreed, and ornithologists reclassified them as one species.

When and Where to See Them: In coniferous and mixed forests of canyons and mountains of Arizona, New Mexico, southern Utah, and southwestern Colorado, spring through fall; in southeastern California and far western Texas in winter. Year-round in parts of southern Arizona.

Eyecatchers

Be on the lookout for a fluttering of charcoal, yellow, and white among the pines.

Yellow-rumped warbler. –TOM J. ULRICH

Painted Redstart

Myioborus pictus
Family: Warbler

A small black bird, the painted redstart has a bright red patch extending from the lower breast across the belly, and white wing patches and tail edges.

Natural History: You hear a rustling in a sycamore tree and look up to see a busy patch of black, red, and white moving among the foliage—a painted redstart. These boldly colored birds enliven any outing among the forested canyons and valleys of the mountains of central and southern Arizona, at elevations from 5,000 to 7,000 feet. These moist, wooded canyons are a treasure to find amid the arid deserts and shrublands of the Southwest, and bright little birds like the redstart are the jewels.

Eating strictly a diet of insects and other invertebrates, redstarts forage among the foliage, busily probing into the folds of bark or wrinkles of leaves. They also flutter out from a perch to snag flying insects, fanning their tails in a sudden display of black and white. In spring the male pursues the female in a ragged courtship flight, the two of them flashing among the foliage like black, white, and red semaphores. Listen for the rich, clear warbling song of the male; sometimes the female will join him in a duet. They build their nest of grass and pine needles on the ground, concealed on a slope under a rock or shrub, or beneath an overhang.

When and Where to See Them: April through October in canyons and wooded valleys of central to southern Arizona, southwestern New Mexico, and far western Texas.

Eyecatchers

This busy warbler brightly painted red, black, and white flits among the vegetation.

172

Painted redstart. –R. AND N. BOWERS/VIREO

Dark-eyed Junco
A.K.A.: snow bird, mountain junco

Junco hyemalis
Family: Finch

Two of the four races of dark-eyed junco are prominent in the Southwest. The Oregon form has a dark, blue-gray hood covering its head and upper chest, rust red back and sides, and gray wings and tail. The gray-headed has a light gray head and sides and reddish brown back. All juncos have white-edged tails.

Natural History: The dark-eyed junco demonstrates how the natural world cannot be easily and neatly categorized. Not long ago the four very different-looking races of dark-eyed junco were all thought to be different species. Then those rascals interbred, forcing biologists to reclassify them all as one species.

In the Southwest, we mainly see the dark-hooded **Oregon junco** and the gray-hooded, red-backed **gray-headed junco**. If you see a gray-headed junco with a definite yellow eye (and you are in southeastern Arizona), you are seeing an entirely different species, the **yellow-eyed junco.** If all this seems confusing, don't feel bad. The important thing is to enjoy watching these bright, handsome, very visible birds who enliven mountain forests in summer and lower elevations in winter.

Juncos are ground feeders; you may notice them in winter picking up seeds that have fallen beneath your bird feeders. In the woods, a foraging flock of juncos spreads out, searching for seeds and berries, keeping in touch by calling constantly with a terse *tsik*. They are so well adapted to life on the ground that the legs of the nestlings develop rapidly, allowing them to flee danger by running before they can fly.

When and Where to See Them: Throughout the Southwest in lower foothills, canyons, and at backyard feeders in winter; moving into higher-elevation coniferous forests and mixed woodlands in mountains and canyons mid-April to mid-October.

Eyecatchers

A busy gray bird forages about the floor of a mountain forest, wearing a cowl of bluish charcoal or gray. Look for the dark smudge around the "Bette Davis eyes."

Dark-eyed junco, gray-headed race. —JIM CLARK

Dark-eyed junco, Oregon race. —JIM CLARK

—JIM CLARK

Southwest Birding Hotspots

The Southwest is home to birdwatching destinations of national and international renown. Southeastern Arizona, in particular, encompasses some of the best birding sites in the country.

Arizona

Grand Canyon National Park. Particularly good for raptors, mountain, and canyon birds and birds typical of the Colorado Plateau.

Cave Creek Canyon, Portal. Known for trogons, hummingbirds, and songbirds. Some biologists claim this site has the richest diversity of wildlife in the United States.

Arizona-Sonora Desert Museum, Tucson. The captive collection of regional birds is impressive, and the wild "freeloaders" inhabiting this open-air park are fun to watch.

Patagonia-Sonoita Creek Preserve, Patagonia. Great diversity of riparian and open woodland species. More than 250 species of birds recorded.

Madera Canyon, Green Valley. Variety of songbirds, warblers, hummingbirds, and border specialties, such as trogons. Over 200 bird species recorded here.

Ramsey Canyon, Sierra Vista. Renowned for hummingbirds in spring and summer. Also an abundance of songbirds.

Saguaro National Monument, Tucson. Excellent for desert and shrubland birds; also mountain birds in the Rincon Mountain district of the monument.

New Mexico

Bosque del Apache National Wildlife Refuge, Socorro. Sandhill cranes and snow geese in winter. Great variety of waterfowl, shore and wading birds, and raptors.

Rattlesnake Springs, Carlsbad. Over 300 species recorded here.

Manzano Mountains HawkWatch, Manzano. Excellent for migrating fall raptors. Hundreds of raptors are seen daily at the season's peak.

California

Salton Sea, Indio. Wading and shorebirds, waterfowl.

Anza-Borrego Desert State Park, Borrego Springs. California desert habitat and palm oases. Desert and shrubland birds; more than 200 birds on the bird list.

Texas

Big Bend National Park. Desert and mountain species, raptors, hummingbirds, and border specialties. A premier wildlife viewing area, with over 400 bird species recorded.

Suggested Reading

National Geographic Society Field Guide to the Birds of North America. Shirley L. Scott, editor. Washington, D.C.: National Geographic Society. 1991.

A Field Guide to Western Birds. Roger Tory Peterson. Boston: Houghton Mifflin Company. 1990.

Arizona Wildlife Viewing Guide. John N. Carr. Helena, Mont.: Falcon Press. 1992.

New Mexico Wildlife Viewing Guide. Jane MacCarter. Helena, Mont.: Falcon Press. 1992.

Birder's Guide to Southeastern Arizona. Harold R. Holt. Colorado Springs, Colo.: American Birding Association. 1989.

A New Mexico Birdfinding Guide. Dale Zimmerman, editor. Albuquerque: New Mexico Ornithological Society. 1992.

Seasonal Guide to the Natural Year—Colorado, New Mexico, Arizona and Utah. Ben Guterson. Golden, Colo.: Fulcrum Publishing. 1994.

The Great Southwest Nature Factbook. Susan J. Tweit. Bothell, Wash.: Alaska Northwest Books. 1992.

Shrubs and Trees of the Southwest Uplands. Francis H. Elmore. Tucson, Ariz.: Southwest Parks and Monuments Association. 1976.

Shrubs and Trees of the Southwest Deserts. Janice Emily Bowers. Tucson, Ariz.: Southwest Parks and Monuments Association. 1993.

The Audubon Society Encyclopedia of North American Birds. John K. Terres. New York: Wings Books. 1991.

The Audubon Society Nature Guides—Deserts. James A. MacMahon. New York: Alfred A. Knopf. 1994.

Photograph Credits and Copyrights

Photographs © 1995 Robert E. Barber: pages 53 and 73.

Photographs © 1995 Paul A. Berquist: page 151 and back cover.

Photograph © 1995 Paul Berquist: page 79 (bottom).

Photographs © 1995 Paul and Shirley Berquist: pages 75, 89, and front cover (quail).

Photograph © 1995 Shirley Berquist: page 77 (bottom).

Photograph © 1995 R. and N. Bowers/VIREO: page 173.

Photograph © 1995 Jim Clark: pages 1, 15 (top), 17 (bottom), 19, 21, 23 (bottom), 25, 29 (top), 31 (top), 33 (top), 37, 41 (top and center), 43, 45, 47 (top), 57, 63, 111 (bottom), 117 (top), 119 (bottom), 121, 127 (bottom), 129 (top), 135, 155, 165 (bottom), 167, and 175.

Photograph © 1995 H. Clarke/VIREO: page 149.

Photographs © 1995 Chris Geanious: pages 5 (bottom), 51 (bottom), and 97 (top).

Photographs © 1995 Mary Taylor Gray: pages 2, 3, 5 (top), 8, 12, 27, 33 (center and bottom), 41 (bottom), 59, 60, 69, 79 (top), 81, 83, 101 (bottom), 103 (bottom), 109, 113 (bottom), 119 (top), 131, 133, 136, 157, 161, 169, 176, and front cover (landscape).

Photograph © 1995 Cathy and Gordon Illg: page 115 (top).

Photographs © 1995 Bryan H. Pridgeon: pages 15 (bottom), 17 (top), 23 (top and center), 31 (bottom), 47 (bottom), 55, 67, 93, 95, and 117 (bottom).

Photographs © 1995 Steve Renzi: pages 77 (top), 103 (top), 111 (top), 113 (top), and 147.

Photographs © 1995 Wendy Shattil/Bob Rozinski: pages 39, 49, 71, 99, 101 (center), 105, 107, 123, 143, 145, and 165 (top).

Photographs © 1995 Tom J. Ulrich: pages 51 (top), 101 (top), 125, 159, and 171.

Photographs © 1995 Jan L. Wassink: pages 91, 115 (bottom), 153, and 163 (bottom).

Photographs © 1995 Terry Wygant: pages 29 (bottom), 35, 65, 85, 87, 127 (top), 129 (bottom), 139, and 141.

Photograph © 1995 Richard K. Young: page 187.

Photographs © 1995 D. and M. Zimmerman/VIREO: pages 97 (bottom) and 163 (top).

Index

Acoma Indians, 166
Aeronautes saxatalis, 148
Agelaius phoeniceus, 54
American Vulture Family, 62
Amphispiza bilineata, 124
Anas acuta, 30
Anas crecca, 26
Anas cyanoptera, 32
Anas platyrhynchos, 27
Anasazi, 144
Anza-Borrego Desert State Park, x, 178
Aphelocoma ultramarina, 156
Aquila chrysaetos, 138
Arches National Park, x, 9
Archilochus alexandri, 98
Ardea herodias, 16
Arizona-Sonora Desert Museum,
    161, 177

Bald Eagle Act, 138
Bandelier National Monument, 9
Bee Bird, 58
Big Bend National Park, x, 9, 178
Black-chin, 98
Black-throat, 124
Blackbird
    Brewer's, 54
    Crow, 130
    Marsh, 54
    Red-winged, 13, 54-57
    Yellow-headed, 54
Blue Peter, 40
Blue Pop, 122
Blue Rail, 40
Bluebird
    Eastern, 168
    Mexican, 168
    Mountain, 168
    Western, 137, 168-69
Bosque Del Apache National Wildlife
    Refuge, x, 3, 22, 23, 42, 177
Branta canadensis, 24
Bryce Canyon National Park, x, 9

Bubo virginianus, 84
Bugler, 166
Bullfinch, 120
Butcher Bird, 116
Buteo jamaicensis, 62
Butorides virescens, 20

Callipepla gambelii, 74
Callipepla squamata, 72
Calypte costae, 100
Campylorhynchus brunneicapillus, 108
Canyon de Chelly National Monument,
    x, 9, 142, 144
Canyonlands National Park, x, 9
Capitol Reef National Park, x, 9
Cardinal
    Gray, 120
    Northern, 61, 118-19, 120
Cardinalis cardinalis, 118
Cardinalis sinuatus, 120
Carlsbad Caverns National Park, x, 9
Carpodacus mexicanus, 134
Carrion Crow, 62
Cathartes aura, 62
Catherpes mexicanus, 16
Cave Creek Canyon, 177
Ceryle alcyon, 48
Chaco Culture National Historic Park,
    x, 9, 144
Charadrius vociferus, 46
Chen caerulescens, 22
Chickadee, Black-capped, 162, 163
Chiricahua National Monument, 9
Chordeiles acutipennis, 94
Circus cyaneus, 38
Columbina inca, 76
Condor, California, 62
Coot, American, 40, 41
Correo del camino, 80
Corvus corax, 158
Cotton-picker, 116
Cottontop, 72
Cowbird, Brown-headed, 54, 122

Crane
  Blue, 16, 42
  Brown, 42
  Sandhill, 1, 3, 13, 42-45
  Turkey, 42
Crane Family, 42
Crow Family, 154, 156, 158
Cuckoo Family, 80
Curlytail, 28
Cyanocitta stelleri, 154

Dabchick, 14
Dendroica coronata, 170
Devil-down-head, 164
Distraction display, 46
Dove
  Inca, 61, 76-77
  Long-tailed, 76
  Mourning, 61, 78-79
  Scaled, 76
  Turtle, 78
  White-winged, 78
  Wood, 78
Duck
  Gray, 30
  Muscovy, 28
  Pheasant, 30
  Ruddy, 32
Duck Family, 22, 24, 26, 28, 30, 32

Eagle
  American, 34
  Bald, 13, 34-37, 144
  Golden, 34, 137, 138-141
  Mountain, 138
  Ring-tailed, 138
  Royal, 138
  Washington, 34
  White-headed, 34
Egret
  Cattle, 18, 19
  Snowy, 13, 18, 19
Egretta thula, 18
Eremophila alpestris, 106

Falco peregrinus, 142
Falco sparverius, 70
Falcon
  Peregrine, 137, 142-43
  Wandering, 142
Falcon Family, 70, 142
Finch
  House, 61, 134-35
  Mexican House, 134
  Rose-breasted, 134
Finch Family, 118, 120, 122, 124, 126,

134, 174
Flicker, Gilded, 102
Flycatcher
  Black, 114
  Black-headed, 50
  Vermilion, 13, 52-53

Gallinula chloropus, 40
Gallinule, Common, 40
Geococcyx californianus, 80
Glen Canyon National Recreation Area
  (Lake Powell), x, 9
Gobbler, 144
Goose
  Blue, 22, 23
  Canada, 6, 13, 22, 24-25
  Snow, 1, 13, 22-23
Grackle, Great-tailed, 61, 130-31
Grand Canyon National Park, x, 9, 142, 177
Grebe
  Pied-billed, 13, 14-15
  Western, 14
Grebe Family, 14
Greenhead, 28
Greenwing, 26
Grosbeak, Blue, 61, 122-23
Grunt and Whistle Display, 28
Grus canadensis, 42
Guadalupe Mountains National Park, x, 9
Guiraca caerulea, 122

Halcyon, 48
Haliaeetus leucocephalus, 34
Harrier, Northern, 13, 38-39
Hawk
  Duck, 142
  Grasshopper, 70
  Hen, 66
  Marsh, 38
  Mouse, 70
  Red-tailed, 5, 6, 61, 66-69
  Sparrow, 70
Hawk Family, 34, 38, 66, 138
Head-up, Tail-up Display, 28
Hell Diver, 14
Heron
  Great Blue, 13, 16-17
  Green, 13, 20-21
  Green-backed, 20
  Little White, 18
Heron Family, 16, 18, 20
Hirundo pyrrhonota, 152, 153
Hispanics, 80
Honker, 24
Hopi Indians, 96
Hummer, 100

182

Hummingbird
    Anna's, 100
    Black-chinned, 61, 98-99
    Broad-tailed, 100
    Costa's, 61, 100, 101
    Ruby-throated, 98
Hummingbird Family, 98, 100

Inciting Display, 28
Icterus cucullatus, 132

Jackdaw, 130
Jay
    Arizona, 156
    Gray-breasted, 137, 156-57
    Mexican, 156
    Mountain Blue, 154
    Pinyon, 154
    Scrub, 156
    Steller's, 137, 154-55
John Crow, 62
Joshua Tree National Park, x, 9
Junco hyemalis, 174
Junco
    Dark-eyed, 137, 174-75
    Gray-headed, 174, 175
    Mountain, 174
    Oregon, 174, 175
    Yellow-eyed, 174

Kestrel, American, 61, 70-71
Killdee, 46
Killdeer, 13, 46-47
Kingbird
    Arkansas, 104
    Cassin's, 104
    Western, 61, 104-5
Kingfisher, Belted, 48-49

Lake Mead National Recreation Area, x, 9
Lanius ludovicianus, 116
Lark
    Horned, 61, 106-7
    Snow, 106
Lark family, 106
Larking, 106
Lazybird, 48
Little Snowy, 18
Lizard Bird, 80

Madera Canyon, 177
Mallard, 6, 13, 26, 28-29, 30, 32, 33
Manzano Mountains HawkWatch, 177
Meadowlark
    Eastern, 128
    Western, 61, 128-29

Melanerpes formicivorus, 150
Melanerpes uropygialis, 102
Meleagris gallopavo, 144
Mesa Verde National Park, x, 9, 142, 144
Micrathene whitneyi, 88
Mimus polyglottos, 110
Mocker, 110
Mockingbird, Northern, 61, 110-11,
    112, 116
Mockingbird Family, 110, 112
Moorhen, Common, 13, 40-41
Myioborus pictus, 172

Native Americans, 62, 80, 138, 146, 158
Natural Bridges National Monument, x, 9
Night-heron, Black-crowned, 20
Nighthawk
    Common, 94
    Lesser, 61, 94-95
    Trilling, 94
Nightjar Family, 94, 96
Nine-killer, 116
Nuthatch
    Pygmy, 164
    Red-breasted, 164
    White-breasted, 137, 164-65
Nuthatch Family, 164

Organ Pipe Cactus National Monument,
    x, 9
Oriole
    Hooded, 61, 132-33
    Northern, 132
    Palm, 132
    Scott's, 132
Osprey, 34
Owl
    Billy, 90
    Burrowing, 61, 90-93
    Cat, 84
    Elf, 61, 88-89
    Great Horned, 61, 84-87
    Ground, 90
    Hoot, 84
    Howdy, 90
    Whitney's, 90
Owl Family, 84, 88, 90

Paisano, 80
Parrot-bill, 120
Parus wollweberi, 162
Patagonia-Sonoita Creek Preserve, 177
Pewee, Western Black, 50
Phainopepla, 61, 114-15
Phainopepla nitens, 114
Phalaenoptilus nuttallii, 96

Pheasant Family, 72, 74
Phoebe, Black, 13, 50-51
Picket-tail, 30
Pigeon Family, 76, 78
Pintail, Northern, 30-31
Pirangra rubra, 58
Plover, Meadow, 46
Plover Family, 46
Podilymbus podiceps, 14
Poorwill
    Common, 61, 96-97
    Dusky, 96
Pueblo peoples, 32, 62
Pueblo, Picuris, 42
Pyrocephalus rubinus, 52
Pyrrhuloxia, 61, 120-21

Quail
    Arizona, 74
    Blue, 72
    Desert, 74
    Gambel's, 1, 16, 74-75
    Scaled, 61, 72-73
    Topknot, 72
Quiscalus mexicanus, 130

Rail Family, 40
Rattlesnake Springs, 177
Ramsey Canyon, 177
Raven
    American, 158
    Chihuahuan, 158, 161
    Common, 5, 137, 158-61
    White-necked, 158
Red-head, 134
Redbird, 58, 118
Redhead, 32
Redstart, Painted, 137, 172-73
Redtail, 66
Redwing, 54
Roadrunner, Greater, 3, 61, 80-83

Saguaro Cactus, 2, 5, 8, 88, 89, 102, 113
Saguaro National Monument, x, 9, 177
Salton Sea, 178
Sayornis nigricans, 50
Sea Wigeon, 30
Shining Fly-snapper, 114
Shrike, Loggerhead, 61, 116-17
Shrike Family, 116
Sialia mexicana, 168
Silky Flycatcher Family, 114
Sitta carolinensis, 164
Snow Bird, 174
Sonoran Desert, 2, 4, 102

Sparrow
    Black-throated, 61, 124-25
    Desert, 124
    Gambel's, 126
    White-crowned, 61, 126-27
Speotyto cunicularia, 90
Sprig Tail, 30
Sturnella neglecta, 128
Swallow
    Barn, 152
    Cliff, 137, 152-53
    Crescent, 152
    Mud, 152
    Rough-winged, 152
    Tree, 152
    Violet-green, 149, 152
Swallow Family, 152
Swift, White-throated, 137, 148-49
Swift Family, 148

Tanager
    Hepatic, 58
    Summer, 13, 58-59
    Western, 58
Tanager Family, 58
Teal
    Blue-winged, 32
    Cinnamon, 13, 32-33
    Common, 26
    Green-winged, 13, 26-27
    Mud, 26
    Red, 32
    Red-headed, 26
    River, 32
Tewa Indian, 72
Thrasher
    Curve-billed, 61, 112-13
    Palmer's, 112
Thrush Family, 168
Thrush, Mimic, 110
Titmouse
    Bridled, 137, 162-63
    Wollweber's, 162
Titmouse Family, 162
Topsy-turvy Bird, 164
Toxostoma curvirostre, 112
Tree Mouse, 164
Troupial Family, 54, 128, 130, 132
Turkey
    Tom, 144
    Wild, 137, 144-47
    Wood, 144
Turkey Buzzard, 62
Turkey Family, 144
Tyrannus verticalis, 104
Tyrant Flycatcher Family, 50, 52, 104

Vulture, Turkey, 61, 62-65

Warbler
    Audubon's, 170
    Calico, 58
    Grace's, 170
    Lucy's, 170
    Myrtle, 170
    Yellow-rumped, 137, 170-71
Warbler Family, 170, 172
Water Chicken, 40
Water Witch, 14
White Sands National Monument, x, 9
Whip-poor-will, 96
White-crown, 126
Winged Tiger, 84

Woodpecker
    Ant-eating, 150
    Acorn, 137, 150-51
    Gila, 61, 102-3
    Ladder-backed, 102
    Saguaro, 102
Woodpecker Family, 102, 150
Wren, Brown-headed Cactus
    Cactus, 61, 108-9
    Canyon, 137, 166-67
    Dotted, 166
Wren Family, 108, 166

Zenaida macroura, 78
Zion National Park, x, 9
Zonotrichia leucophrys, 126
Zuñi, 106, 150, 158

The author with two long-time outdoors compadres—Margo (right) and Cody.
–RICHARD K. YOUNG

About the Author

Mary Taylor Gray, a professional wildlife and nature writer, has written three books, including *Watchable Birds of the Rocky Mountains* (Mountain Press), plus hundreds of newspaper and magazine articles about wildlife and nature. Her column on birdwatching, "Words on Birds," appears monthly in the *Rocky Mountain News*. A biologist with a degree in zoology, she edits and writes for *Colorado's Wildlife Company*, a quarterly publication of the Colorado Division of Wildlife. An avid hiker, camper, wildlife watcher, and conservationist, Gray lives in Denver with her husband and many wild avian neighbors.

We encourage you to patronize your local bookstores. Most stores will order any title that they do not stock. You may also order directly from Mountain Press by mail, using the order form provided below or by calling our toll-free number and using your Visa or MasterCard. We will gladly send you a complete catalog upon request.

Some other Natural History titles of interest:

____A Guide to Rock Art Sites Southern California and Southern Nevada	$20.00
____Alpine Wildflowers of the Rocky Mountains	$14.00
____Beachcombing the Atlantic Coast	$15.00
____Birds of the Central Rockies	$14.00
____Birds of the Northern Rockies	$12.00
____Birds of the Pacific Northwest Mountains	$14.00
____Coastal Wildflowers of the Pacific Northwest	$14.00
____Edible and Medicinal Plants of the West	$21.00
____Graced by Pines The Ponderosa Pine in the American West	$10.00
____Hollows, Peepers, and Highlanders An Appalachian Mountain Ecology	$14.00
____An Introduction to Northern California Birds	$14.00
____An Introduction to Southern California Birds	$14.00
____The Lochsa Story Land Ethics in the Bitterroot Mountains	$20.00
____Mammals of the Central Rockies	$14.00
____Mammals of the Northern Rockies	$12.00
____Mountain Plants of the Pacific Northwest	$20.00
____New England's Mountain Flowers	$17.00
____Northwest Weeds The Ugly and Beautiful Villains of Fields, Gardens, and Roadsides	$14.00
____OWLS Whoo are they?	$12.00
____Plants of Waterton-Glacier National Parks and the Northern Rockies	$12.00
____Roadside Plants of Southern California	$15.00
____Sagebrush Country A Wildflower Sanctuary	$14.00
____Watchable Birds of the Southwest	$14.00

Please include $3.00 per order to cover shipping and handling.

Send the books marked above. I enclose $_____

Name_____

Address_____

City_____State_____Zip_____

☐ Payment enclosed (check or money order in U.S. funds)
Bill my: ☐ VISA   ☐ MasterCard   Expiration Date:_____

Card No._____

Signature_____

Mountain Press Publishing Company
P.O. Box 2399 • Missoula, MT 59806
Order Toll Free 1-800-234-5308
Have your Visa or MasterCard ready.